LINDA BARKER'S
Stamping Kit

Photography by Lizzie Orme

Little, Brown and Company
Boston • New York • London

For Chris and Jessica

A LITTLE, BROWN BOOK
First published in Great Britain in 1997
by Little, Brown and Company (UK)
This paperback edition first published in 2001

Text and designs copyright © Eddison Sadd Editions 1997
Photographs copyright © Lizzie Orme 1997 (except page 7)
This edition copyright © Eddison Sadd Editions 2001

A CIP catalogue record for this book is available from the British Library.

ISBN 0-316-85728-9

1 3 5 7 9 8 6 4 2

AN EDDISON•SADD EDITION
Edited, designed and produced by
Eddison Sadd Editions Limited
St Chad's House
148 King's Cross Road
London WC1X 9DH

Phototypeset in Modern MT Extended, Caslon Open Face and Shelley Volante.
Colour origination by Chroma Graphics (Overseas) Pte Ltd Singapore.
Printed and bound by Donnelley Bright Sun, China.

Little, Brown and Company (UK)
Brettenham House
Lancaster Place
London WC2E 7EN

CONTENTS

INTRODUCTION

Linda

All of us want to make our living spaces desirable – it is one of the things that makes home decorating such a challenge. Should we colour wash the walls or rag roll them? Is the kitchen large enough to incorporate that charming old dresser we've always wanted? There are endless ways to style and decorate our homes and there are many inspiring interior features in books and magazines from which we can take ideas. When you are thinking about starting to decorate a room in your home, first gather together all those imaginative books, pictures and magazine cuttings and spread them out over the floor in front of you (preferably in the room where you are working) and try to determine just what it was about those images that you liked so much. Look at colours and styles and imagine them on your own walls. Assess the different paint effects and weigh these up against the effect that a plain, flat colour has on a room. If you like the stamping effect in the Living Room chapter of this book *(see pages 60–65)*, but you prefer the colourway used in the bedroom, well, simply adapt the colours to suit your own requirements. Why not use the duck egg blue shade seen on the dressing table in the Bedroom chapter of this book *(see pages 74–79)* to colour the walls and then stamp, using the blocks seen on the wall of the living room? The choice is yours.

Stamping can be great fun and the results are unbelievably quick – you could complete a room within a day and a piece of furniture in a matter of hours. It is quite by surprise that I find myself to be an avid stamping enthusiast. Although the craft of stamping is a relatively new phenomenon, it can soon become rather addictive. Show me a plain surface and I will, rather compulsively, stamp on it! Apart from those very early attempts at stamping during formative kindergarten years, using lumps of potato and messy powder colours, I had never really given much thought to stamping. That was, of course, until I spotted one of those tiny wooden printing blocks in my local art suppliers. With a quick press of the printing block onto an ink pad, which was then transferred onto a surface, it couldn't have been much easier. My thoughts were then transferred to the idea of the stamped effect on furniture and fabrics. Mind you, the price of one tiny block soon thwarted any desire that I may have had to buy up a whole armful of blocks, but it inspired me to have a go at making my own. As a result of this experimentation, over the next few pages you will find out exactly how you can make your own stamping blocks for just a fraction of the cost of those on sale in the shops using the stamp designs featured at the back of this book *(see pages 118–125)* or your own unique ideas.

THE ORIGINS OF DECORATIVE PAPERS AND HAND-BLOCKING

Long before the advent of wallpapers or decorative painting, bare walls in palaces, castles, villas and large houses belonging to wealthy Europeans would have been covered in tapestries or sometimes painted cloth. Wood panelling or leather work would also have been used for decoration. However, with the introduction of paper making in the late fifteenth century, a less expensive form of decoration was created, in the shape of wallpaper. These early papers would all have been hand painted or stencilled. Later on, decorative techniques that evolved in the seventeenth century led to the block printing technique, which allowed greater quantities of paper to be produced in much faster time than ever before.

Extravagant papers emulated the luxurious tapestries and silk wall hangings, using both block printing and also a flocking technique. Fashionable flocked wallpapers were made by dusting powdered fibres over a slow-drying adhesive that was applied to the paper and these were unequivocally *de rigueur* in the seventeenth century. At the same time, the Chinese produced a range of fine decorative papers using etched plates or woodblocks. The colour was applied either by stencil or by hand and many of these papers have survived to this day. Images of printed panoramic scenes and country landscapes, architectural columns and capitals all appeared in France in the later part of the eighteenth century. These wall coverings were so intricate and precise in style that they needed specialist hanging.

At first the early papers were quite expensive but, by the beginning of the nineteenth century, the walls in an average room could be papered for a price that was the equivalent of a day's wage, which made papers much cheaper than paints. People then began to use papers for decorating in greater quantities, not only to provide a visual richness, but also to reduce the flow of dampness and draughts coming through their walls. At this time, many inexpensive papers were produced, but unfortunately the quality of papers started to decay and so they began to lose their general popularity.

It was not until recently that walls painted in a solid colour were a common sight, due to the high cost of the work and because the paints stained easily. The relatively new DIY movement has changed the face of home design. New paints and easy-to-use products all contribute to easing what was once the drudgery of home decorating and never before has it been so accessible to so many.

At first I was rather curious to know exactly how a stamp could be used to decorate large areas, such as the entire wall surface in a room. My first attempts at stamping were very encouraging and my conclusion was, of course, that stamps are a brilliant way of creating an 'all-over effect' and are much simpler to use than stencils, which require careful alignment. When building up an

The block store at Arthur Sanderson & Sons (top), *where sets of wooden blocks for 340 different designs are carefully stacked. These include the Acanthus design* (below) *created by William Morris in 1875, which is still available today.*

all-over pattern, stencils do require more of an artistic skill, whereas stamps are far more immediate and so much easier to control.

For many years, stencils have been used to emulate the effects of exquisite, but expensive wallpapers, particularly when wallpapers were first produced by skilled craftsmen. And the technique of stamping too, can be used to recreate these effects with great success. Historically, the printing process used to create those wonderful old hand-blocked papers was, in fact, achieved with huge wooden printing blocks that were lowered onto plain paper fitted onto grand printing presses. At first the block was charged with the colour and then lowered carefully over the roll of paper using the registration marks for precise alignment. Each colour needed a separate printing block, and more intricate papers required several blocks in order to make up their pattern. As you can imagine, the cost was prohibitively expensive for most people, but the stunning beauty and intricate craftsmanship that went into these papers was inevitably reflected in their cost. Some of the original blocks are still in existence today and these are used by the producers of fine wallpapers, although you can expect to pay a princely sum for them. The exceptional quality of hand-blocked papers doesn't come cheap: cost is directly related to the quality of materials, rich colours and the sheer length of time that it takes a skilled craftsworker to produce such a glorious product. Today, in a similar, but far humbler way, we are looking to capture the unique effect of this hand-blocked quality with our own printing blocks.

USING STAMPS TO ACHIEVE A HAND-BLOCKED EFFECT

You will soon discover that quite detailed motifs can be cut from soft foam rubber to produce intricate shapes and patterns. Stamping produces a cruder, but no less effective imitation of hand-blocking that can then (rather more affordably) be recreated in our own homes to achieve, if not the same quality of old hand-blocked paper, something that is, without doubt, far more desirable than some of the more garish, mass-produced modern wallpapers on offer in decorating stores.

Like the hand-blocking technique that was used all those years ago, a good stamping effect requires careful registration of the block to line up the pattern of the design and a strong, even pressure is applied to the back of the block to transfer the paint evenly. With the technique of stamping, we are not necessarily able to recreate those wonderful old wallpaper designs, but we can

certainly use them for inspiration in the hope of making an interesting design for ourselves that achieves a bold impact and for very little outlay.

An interesting effect that appears on the surface of the stamped design, characteristic of the hand-blocking technique, is the slightly dimpled surface of the paint. This happens when a block is lifted away from the surface upon which the block has been set and the effect is a result of the paint lifting ever so slightly as the block is pulled away from the flat surface. Dimpling sometimes occurs on hand-blocked papers too and is a particularly charming characteristic of the stamped motif, whether it appears on an expensive paper or on our own, (and perhaps rather more humbly-printed), stamp designs.

In this book, I'll show you how to draw up your own image for a stamping block (if you're feeling creative) or you could simply choose to use one of the outlines that we have provided at the back of this book *(see pages 118–125)*. As is often the case, some of the simplest outlines can look as equally stunning as the more elaborate and more complicated designs. So a simply drawn heart or star motif can be quickly sketched out (even by those who are more artistically challenged) to produce some great results.

CREATING YOUR OWN STAMPING BLOCK

Once you have decided on your outline, trace the design onto a piece of white paper and decide whether this will need to be enlarged or reduced on a photocopier. It is often easiest to start with a small stamp design at first as the block is simpler to control when printing. This advice particularly applies when working on vertical surfaces or larger pieces of furniture. Once your outline is the right size, cut away the excess paper. Use a small amount of spray mount (in a well-ventilated room) to provide a 'just tacky' surface to hold the paper outline onto the piece of foam rubber. If you apply too much spray, it will be difficult to peel away the paper from the foam rubber later on once the outline has been cut. However, too little spray will not hold the sheet in place. Spray mount can be expensive so, rather than purchasing a new can for this purpose alone, you can just as easily hold the template in place using ordinary dressmaker's pins that are simply pushed through the paper into the foam rubber. Use a small pair of scissors or a sharp craft knife to cut around the design (I often use a scalpel blade as these are inexpensive and rechargeable). You will find that the foam cuts away easily, but take care when cutting around the smaller, more intricate parts of your designs. Make sure the blade is at a right angle to the surface so as not to undercut the design and hold the blade at a right angle to the foam.

You will find that the more square the cut of your sawn piece of timber, the easier your task of correctly aligning and printing the stamped design will be. Use a metal right angle (if you have one) to mark out a perfect square and score the lines in dark blue pencil before sawing. If your tool kit doesn't harbour anything that even remotely resembles a right angle, then line up your measurements with the corner of a piece of paper, a book or you could even use a compact disc case. All of these items possess neat, perfect right angles. The size of your block is determined by the size of image that you decide to use. Once you have traced off your design and enlarged or reduced it on a photocopier, use a ruler to measure out both the length and width of the image accurately, and remember that it may either be square or rectangular. The image should fit neatly inside the block, with the edges of the design just touching the sides of the block.

I often use MDF (medium-density fibreboard) for making blocks as it is strong, as well as being easy to cut and it does not warp. Always remember to wear a protective face mask when sawing MDF as its tiny dust particles should not be inhaled – dust will float everywhere, especially if you are using a jigsaw. However, almost any material could be used for a block, provided it is easy to saw and thick enough to hold between your fingertips at the sides. In my own anxiety to get started, I have been known to saw up bits of old skirting board for my blocks, as a trip to the timber merchant seemed just too far and this has worked out perfectly well! Indeed, for the tiny black stamps that were printed onto the tiled splashback featured in the Bathroom chapter *(refer to pages 92–95)*, I used one of the tiny mosaic tiles to make the actual block. However, this particular project was an exception and, when sawing timber to make up the blocks, you must first carefully align the cutting edge of the saw with the marked lines. Cut the timber and smooth down any rough edges using abrasive paper to create a perfect block that is ready for the foam rubber to be applied.

Make sure you transfer the drawn image of the design onto both surfaces of the block (you will soon discover that the outlines on one side of the block are critical for correct alignment of the pieces of foam rubber). The outline you have traced onto the other side of the block will help you to position it correctly when stamping onto a surface as you won't be able to see the underside of the block. Use contact adhesive to secure the foam rubber pieces onto the block, ensuring a perfect bond, and once this is dry you are now ready to begin stamping. Detailed step-by-step photographs and further instructions on the technique of making up a stamp can be found later on *(see pages 32–33)*.

I hope that you will enjoy recreating the projects that I have designed especially for this book and may even feel inspired to start creating your own design motifs to (quite literally) put your own stamp upon your home!

Part One
TECHNIQUES

This section of the book outlines all the techniques that you will need to get going with your stamping projects. It provides you with detailed step-by-step instructions for the most commonly used paint finishes to be used in conjunction with the stamped designs. Within these pages you will also find out how to make up your own stamping block and, more importantly, how to use it to effect on different surfaces and how to embellish your stamped design once it is printed. You'll also find advice on buying paints, choosing colours and which surfaces to stamp on – everything you could possibly need, in fact, to get started.

MATERIALS AND EQUIPMENT

All the materials and equipment that you really need to start stamping are the basic items, such as scraps of timber, adhesives and emulsion colours, that are generally found in most homes. Foam rubber is the only specialist material that you will need to source from outside. The best suppliers for this will be listed in a local phone directory and some may even have a mail order service. It is generally sold by the metre or yard in 3 mm (⅛ in) sheets. Everything else is quite easy to find and, unlike many other crafts, you do not need to incur any great expense to begin. In fact, long before the more sophisticated wooden block came into its own, there was always the humble potato print, and some of the less complicated motifs, such as stars or hearts, can be printed with a potato. In an effort to just get going, the potato could be your starting point whilst your delivery of foam rubber is on its way from the supplier!

STAMPING BLOCK
Fundamental to beginning, small offcuts of MDF (medium-density fibreboard) or timber are used to make the stamping block. Often a DIY store or timber suppliers will have a stack of offcuts of this type of material so you shouldn't have to pay very much for it. Some places may even give you the offcuts for nothing at all – it really depends on the amount of wood that you require. Ensure that the offcut used is a good thickness, ideally 25 mm (1 in) or more is best as this will enable you to hold the stamp more easily at the sides of the block. Some DIY stores offer a cutting service that is available for a small charge, but you may well find that they are unable to cut small blocks.

FOAM RUBBER
Available in sheets, foam rubber comes from specialist suppliers. It is usually sold in a variety of thicknesses and is generally black in colour. For stamping purposes, thicknesses of 3, 4 or 5 mm (approximately ⅛, ¹¹⁄₆₄ or ¹³⁄₆₄ in) are ideal.

SAWS, ABRASIVE PAPERS AND WIRE WOOL
The timber or MDF that is used for the stamping block is easily cut using a small tenon saw or a jigsaw, if you have one. (Always wear a protective face mask when cutting MDF.) Mark the cutting lines out clearly with a pencil and use a set square or right-angled 'T' square to ensure that the block is cut precisely. Once the block is cut, you will need to smooth off the rough edges. There are many types of abrasive paper (sandpaper) available on the market and they will all do the same job. There's no need to buy in anything specifically for stamping, just use whatever is to hand: rough, coarse or fine – they will all have the same desired effect, which is namely to prevent splinters from getting into your hands! Wire wool is an extremely useful material and again, this comes in a number of very different grades (as does abrasive paper), ranging from coarse to medium and fine. It is often used to distress colours to achieve an antiqued and distressed paint effect, and it can also be used to apply beeswax whenever this type of finish is also required.

CRAFT KNIVES
You will need a very sharp blade (and a cutting mat) to cut cleanly through the foam rubber. A scalpel is the best knife for this and this can be purchased at craft or art suppliers. If you don't have a scalpel blade, a Stanley knife is perfectly acceptable but for the cleanest cut, make sure you use a new blade for cutting. Make sure that you replace this regularly, whenever the blade starts to pull or drag on the foam sheet. Alternatively, small, sharp scissors may be used for cutting the foam, but a sharp cutting edge is essential.

ADHESIVE
For stamping, contact adhesive is the only adhesive to use: no other product can be substituted. It provides the strongest fixing and enables the stamp to be easily cleaned in water after use. Contact adhesive is applied to both surfaces that are to be bonded together: that is, the back of the foam rubber stamp and the top surface of the block. Only when the two glued surfaces are totally dry are the pieces then pressed together to create a strong bond. Press the two surfaces gently together and make sure all the foam has made contact with the block and then it's ready for use.

PAINTS
The kind of paint that you use depends on the type of surface that you are decorating. In general, most of the stamped surfaces in this book

use coloured, water-based emulsion paint. A basic brilliant white emulsion can be tinted using tubes of acrylic colour to reach the desired shade and is the most economical way of creating the perfect colour.

Be methodical in your approach to tinting emulsion colours. Store everything after use: you will find that glass jars are ideal for mixing and keeping paint so that you can then create your own range of colours. Brushes and other items can be cleaned with water after use of emulsions and tinted colours.

Universal stainers (in several colours) may also be used for tinting paints and varnishes. Use an old paintbrush to mix stainers.

OTHER NEEDS

An ordinary piece of window glass, although not critical to stamping by any stretch of the imagination, is well worth obtaining. This is perfect for brushing on a thin layer of paint colour, then pressing your stamp directly onto it for even coverage. Old, chipped dinner plates are also extremely useful for this purpose (if you have them), but if you are using a large stamp then these larger blocks will not fit inside the curved rim of an ordinary plate. Do use masking tape to cover the sides of the glass to protect your hands from the sharp edges.

A can of spray mount is also very useful. This is used to lightly dust the back of a drawn outline, which is then placed onto the foam rubber. The spray adhesive holds the outline in place as a guide for cutting out the rubber. Always use spray in a well ventilated room as the glue particles do tend to float around and could be harmful, if inhaled. If you are using spray mount inside or outside, secure sheets of paper around

all three sides of the work when you are spraying to contain the adhesive.

A hard roller can be used to even out the paint on a glass surface and it can also be used to transfer paint directly onto the block, if necessary.

OTHER PAINTS

I occasionally use artist's colours on some stamping projects, either for embellishing a stamp with a hand-finished detail, such as the dressing table *(see pages 76–79)* or for adding details such as the fine lining on the country style wall unit *(see pages 112–115)*. The nursery project is an example of an occasion where I would always choose to use an artist's colour, principally because I only need a small amount of colour.

Artist's colours are available from all good art suppliers and craft stores. They come in a whole range of different shades and you can also mix and blend the primary colours, if necessary, to obtain more specific hues of colour.

Both artist's acrylic or gouache colours are suitable for use when an artist's colour is required. The acrylic colour has a thicker, more plastic-like quality, which is the type of colour that I would choose to work with on decorating projects.

Glass colours or ceramic paints are specialist types of paint that should always be used on the appropriate surfaces for the best bond between paint and surface. They may have different solvents, such as white or methylated spirits. Always check which is the right solvent according to the manufacturer's instructions on the label.

DIFFERENT VARNISHES

Polyurethane varnish is oil-based and available in several forms. Tins of varnish are available for brushing

onto surfaces and cans are available for spraying. Brushing is more time-consuming and you need to clean up paintbrushes and solvents afterwards. Spraying is quick and easy, but it can be expensive, particularly when working on larger projects.

Brush-on varnish is available in many different colours (usually wood tones), but it can be tinted to any colour using artist's oil colours or universal stainers.

OTHER VARNISHES

These can include crackle varnish, which is actually a two-part system. Different varnishes have different drying times and when applied one over the other, they result in a crazed surface (like the effect seen in many old master paintings). Two-part varnish is available as a two-part water-based varnish, which gives even results every time, or there is a slightly more temperamental oil- and water-based varnish system, which is the most widely available. Make sure you always follow the manufacturer's instructions.

WATER-BASED VERSUS OIL PAINTS

Wherever possible, I try to use water-based paints. These are kinder to the environment and it is quicker and easier to wash equipment and tools in warm, soapy water. Provided your piece of furniture is sufficiently prepared, water-based emulsion has enough 'key' to bond it to the surface. Any items that are subject to heavy wear and tear should be protected with a layer of varnish once the paint is dry.

Oil-based paints should always be used on metal surfaces: drying time increases with these paints and your tools must be washed with white spirit after use.

STAMPING ESSENTIALS

1 Coloured furniture wax
2 Household emulsion brush
3 Paint kettle
4 Abrasive paper
5 Methylated spirits
6 Contact adhesive
7 Assorted blocks
8 Fretsaw
9 Assorted artists' brushes
10 Cellulose decorator's sponges
11 Regular masking tape
12 Low-tack masking tape
13 Beeswax
14 Gilt powder
15 Long-haired paintbrush
16 Wire wool
17 Universal stainers
18 Small, sharp scissors
19 Stanley knife
20 Hard roller
21 Right-angled ruler
22 Sketch pad
23 Foam rubber sheet
24 Scalpel

SURFACES FOR STAMPING

Almost any kind of surface can accept a stamp, provided that you use the correct paint for that particular surface. Always refer to the manufacturer's instructions before you begin. Use fabric paints on textiles, ceramic colours for tiles, and so on. . . . The most commonly stamped surfaces are, of course, walls and furniture. Junk or 'blank' furniture are both appropriate for stamping once they have been suitably prepared for painting. But equally, so are natural cotton, linen and silk fabrics, and ceramic and glass surfaces are also appropriate for stamping, although this is not so generally realized.

JUNK FURNITURE

Scour local junk shops, second-hand stores, car boot (garage) sales, auction rooms and house clearances for great sources of junk furniture. A quick glance will soon determine whether or not the furniture is in a good condition. Turn it over and look underneath, if possible, and don't touch anything with visible signs of woodworm – almost anything else can be repaired, depending on how much renovating you will do.

There are some great bargains to be had in junk shops. Seek out the lesser-known outlets that are away from the main street or visit 'once a week' street markets for the best deals and don't be afraid to haggle.

Undoubtedly, the best pieces are those made from solid wood, as opposed to flimsy veneer or ply, and it is these pieces that will take readily to a paint finish. The pieces that I would generally stay clear of are those that have heavily laminated or varnished surfaces. Modern black, lacquered furniture often turns up as junk and, in my estimation, that is exactly what it is and it should be left alone. I also tend to steer clear of veneered items. Generally, these are 'junked' because their veneer is blistered and it can be quite difficult to rectify this problem once it has occurred. So, unless the piece is very attractive, I would also tend to avoid this type of purchase.

JUNK FURNITURE

Utility furniture, such as this wonderful old armchair, is perfect for renovation. Tables, like the glass-topped one and the beautiful table with elegant barley-twist legs shown here, are great junk finds, as are the sturdy wooden kitchen chairs that were picked up at a local auction for practically nothing at all. And simply-styled cabinets with flat-fronted doors make perfect surfaces to work on and transform with a whole range of decorative effects.

16

BLANK FURNITURE

'Blanks' are a new type of MDF-built furniture that is designed particularly for the home decorator. The furniture is often distributed through mail order companies who often advertise in the *back pages of home interest magazines. Tables, small cabinets, trays, plant holders, magazine and letter racks, candlesticks and screens are all distributed in this way.*

BLANK FURNITURE

Some MDF furniture that is supplied through mail order can arrive as 'flat pack' and will require a simple, quick assembly, generally with nothing more complicated than an allen key and this is usually provided as part of the 'pack'. Other items arrive completely assembled and these require nothing more than a quick wipe over with a cloth before painting. You will inevitably pay a little more for these finished items, but as the furniture is still in its raw state it will still be a considerable saving on finished, painted goods.

I would recommend applying a thin layer of water-based, white acrylic primer prior to the base coat as this provides a good surface for subsequent paint layers to bond onto and it also gives a protection between the base coat and the MDF.

Blank MDF is ideal for painting: its smooth surface is wonderful for almost every paint finish, and the paint goes on easily and effortlessly. In most cases, I use water-based emulsion paint for painting both junk and MDF furniture. If the item is likely to receive a great deal of heavy wear and tear, then the surface is protected with either furniture wax or layers of acrylic varnish. Use ordinary matt emulsion colours as these have far less of a plastic-like quality than the vinyl ranges. The matt surface of the paint is then perfect for stamping onto, and the block has less of a tendency to slide on this surface.

Water-based paints are quite strong and durable enough for most furniture painting and they are, without doubt, the easiest colours to use. Paintbrushes are easily washed in water, as indeed are skin, clothes and carpet splashes, should accidents occur. However, their biggest advantage is that drying times are much faster. Entire projects can often be finished in the same day.

BROKEN COLOUR WORK

Occasionally I will use a scumble glaze to produce a broken colour effect over a solid base coat. Once again, although available in oil- and water-based forms, I tend to work with the water-based equivalent. The glaze appears to be a rather milky-white colour in its container but once dry, it will be transparent.

VARNISHES

For a more durable and protective finish, apply at least two layers of acrylic varnish over the painted and stamped surface. For best results, allow the first layer to dry completely, then rub over this surface lightly with fine grade abrasive paper. Wipe clean and then apply the next coat.

Acrylic varnish can be purchased through most DIY stores. It has an opaque, milky-white look but once again, like scumble glaze, it will dry to a completely transparent finish. This varnish is really tough and hard-wearing: it will not yellow with age and the drying times are also much quicker.

STAMPING ONTO FABRICS

When you think of stamping, almost always the idea of decorating walls and furniture is conjured up. However, with the right paints it is easy to print your own fabrics.

Most art and craft stores now supply a wide range of fabric colours in small jars. These paints are thick and viscous and they shouldn't be confused with the watery silk colours that are used to flood colour onto silk. The colours can be mixed together successfully for softer tones. I tend to purchase the primary colours, plus a white and black, and mix my own shades.

Use these paints in the same way as you would ordinary emulsion colours for stamping onto furniture. Decant a little colour onto a sheet of glass or a flat plate and brush this outwards into a thin layer. Press the stamp into the colour and check to see if the paint has transferred onto the printing surface. If it hasn't, then repeat this procedure until the stamp is loaded correctly, then transfer the colour onto your fabric. You will find it easier to stamp by working on a flat surface. But you must first protect the surface as the paint will pass through the fabric layer. Use masking tape to secure a plastic sheet over the table, then spread sheets of newspaper over this. Next, lay the fabric over the newspaper and tape this into position. Once this area of fabric has been printed, remove the tape and lift the fabric off the table top. Replace the newspaper with clean sheets, then tape the next section of fabric in position. Continue until all the required fabric is stamped. For small pieces of fabric, repeat this process on a smaller scale.

Natural fabrics are best for stamping. Cotton, linen and canvas fabrics all work well and not only in the plain colourways. Stronger fabric paints will stamp successfully over a checked gingham or ticking, particularly if a little white is mixed with the base colour to make the colour more opaque.

Checked fabrics can also be useful for positioning the stamp accurately. For the stamped fabric blinds in the Nursery section of this book (*see page 110*), a small heart motif was printed in alternate squares. One square equalled the size of the printing block, which meant the heart was printed in exactly the same position each time. When printing onto plain fabrics, care must be taken to accurately measure the position of each stamp in order to build up a regular design pattern.

Velvets can also be stamped in the same way, but because of the 'nap' of the cloth, the stamped design will have the appearance of being slightly raised.

STAMPING ONTO FABRICS

A selection of plain and patterned fabrics can all be successfully stamped. Voile or butter muslin, once stamped, can be made up into semi-transparent blinds, which allow light to filter softly into a room, yet still maintain privacy. Strong, washable cottons are perfect for most soft furnishings. The fabric colours are fixed onto the cloth using a hot iron.

GLASS AND CERAMIC SURFACES

Frosted or plain, glass storage bottles are perfect surfaces on which to stamp. Look for those containers with perfectly flat sides, if possible – these square-sided bottles are ideal. Ceramic surfaces should be plain, such as these creamy coloured plates, bowls and jug. Once dry, the special paints available for ceramic and glass are washable but they will not withstand heavy wear and tear in a dishwasher. A simple wipe over with a soapy cloth should suffice.

GLASS AND CERAMICS

GLASS PAINTS

These colours appear to be very dark in their containers but this is because they are transparent and do not contain any white or opaque colourants. The colours are strong, rather like those seen in traditional stained glass. For stamping purposes, I would recommend adding a little bit of white glass paint to the transparent colour to give an opaque quality. The colours are easily mixed together and you may wish to save small, screw-topped glass jars to contain and store colours. The particular solvent used for the glass colours is alcohol-based. For this, I would use methylated spirits, which are usually sold as a bright purple liquid. Use the solvent sparingly as the colours are already quite thin. To clean paintbrushes, first wash them out in the solvent, then finish off in warm, soapy water.

CERAMIC PAINTS

The ceramic colours that are used for stamping are now available in all good art and craft supply stores. Generally, the range of colours should be fairly wide, but it is worth remembering that, as with fabric and glass paints, the ceramic colours can be mixed together to produce your own specific shades.

Before stamping your design onto a glass or ceramic surface, wash the items in hot, soapy water, then wipe them over with a clean, dry cloth. As an additional precaution, wipe the surface with a cloth that has been dampened with a little methylated spirits to completely remove any traces of grease.

You will find it easier to press the stamping block onto a thin layer of paint that has been brushed out onto a sheet of glass. Press the block into the paint, lift it off and check to see if the paint has transferred onto the foam rubber stamp. If not, then press the block into the paint once more to recharge the stamp. When stamping directly onto ceramics or glass, be aware that the surface may be slippery, so apply a firm, even pressure over the block once it is in place on the surface. Finally, lift the block cleanly away from the surface to reveal the stamped design.

If the stamp slips and the print isn't as clear as it should be, then it is preferable to remove the stamped design using a damp, solvent-impregnated cloth and to repeat that particular stamp again. Mistakes can often occur when stamping glass or ceramic surfaces because these surfaces are ultra-smooth and shiny so practise on a sheet of paper first to build up your confidence. Paint colours should be allowed to dry completely before use and, as with the ceramic colours, these items need to be baked in the oven in order to fix the colour firmly onto the surface of the piece. Once the colours are dry, these items can be wiped clean.

PAINT FINISHES

Most painted surfaces will benefit from a soft, dappled surface or a textured finish. And most people will now be familiar with the more commonly used paint finishes that have entered our awareness through numerous decorating books and home interest magazines. Over the last ten years or so, since this decorating phenomenon took a firm hold, we are all probably safe now in the knowledge of how to colour wash, sponge and stencil. And nearly all of us wouldn't blink twice if asked to stipple or rag roll. Paint effects add vitality; they bring a freshness and individuality to everything to which they are applied. Over the next few pages I'll show you some familiar paint finishes and more unusual ones too.

SPONGING

This effect is perhaps the easiest of all the paint finishes. It involves breaking up the underlying base colour using thinned colours applied with a textured sponge. The sponge itself could be a small marine sponge, but it may be more cost-effective to simulate your own sponge from a decorator's cellulose sponge. Cut the rectangular sponge in half, then into quarters (if you are working on smaller projects). Pick out small pieces of sponge to build up a textured surface.

Thin sponging colours with an equal quantity of water and mix thoroughly. Dip the textured surface into the paint and dab the excess off onto scrap paper. Lightly pat the painted surface with the sponge to transfer the paint. Turn the sponge to avoid building up pattern. First sponge a darker colour over the base coat, then a lighter shade and, finally, a layer of white to produce a rather sophisticated, speckled effect.

SPONGING

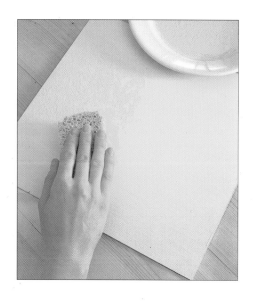

1 Tear small pieces from the cellulose sponge to emulate a natural sea sponge. Dip the sponge into a darker shade of the base colour and then dab this gently over the whole of the painted surface.

2 When the sponged colour is dry (about 30 minutes to an hour), apply a lighter shade over the first one. Turn the sponge occasionally to prevent a pattern building up. Leave to dry for 30 minutes to an hour.

3 Finally, sponge a coat of thinned white emulsion colour over the dried surface, using exactly the same procedure as before. For each colour change, the sponge should be rinsed in water and squeezed dry.

COLOUR RUBBING

Colour rubbing is a simple technique that involves laying a transparent glaze of colour over a dried base coat. The trick here is to rub the glaze over the dried base colour to achieve a rather cloudy effect before the glaze dries, whilst simultaneously removing any excess colour using either a sponge or a dry paintbrush. The finished effect is a wonderfully soft film of colour that allows the underlying colour to show through. When glaze is built up over a blue colour it looks like a perfect cloudy summer sky.

Colour rubbing works particularly well on walls that are to be stamped and on large pieces of furniture, where a flat colour would be too solid (see page 57). For a soft, misty look, mix a glaze that is close in tone to the base colour, perhaps only a few shades paler than the base is all that is needed. Add a little white paint to the base coat colour and work on a test area until you are satisfied with the results.

The glaze coat is made up of one part emulsion colour mixed together with three parts of water-based scumble glaze. At first the glaze will appear to be rather opaque, but the milky glaze dries to a transparent finish. Mix the glaze well in a paint kettle, then apply it over the painted surface using a wide household paintbrush. The glaze extends the drying time of the paint by about an hour, depending on the atmospheric conditions, and helps to achieve a translucent mist of colour.

Once the glaze has been applied, cut a cellulose decorator's sponge into quarters and use one piece to rub over the entire surface of the glaze while it is still wet. Rub the sponge smoothly but firmly across the surface moving outwards in all directions, but following a circular direction. The glaze will slowly start to dry and you will then begin to see the cloudiness building up. Don't overwork the glaze or it may start to streak. Turn the sponge over as excess glaze builds up, and rinse in cool water, as required.

The final effect is reached when the glaze is dry (allow about ten minutes for this depending on the atmosphere), and the paint marks are indistinguishable. Then all that remains is a soft, misty colour.

COLOUR RUBBING

1 Paint a solid base colour over your prepared ground to ensure good coverage. Two coats may be necessary for this and no primer or wood should show through. Leave to dry (about 30 minutes).

2 Mix the glaze colour up according to the proportions mentioned above. Stir thoroughly to amalgamate the paint into the stiff glaze. Brush a layer of this evenly over the dried base coat.

3 Rub the still-wet glaze with a piece of sponge. Work it in a circular scrubbing movement to build up a cloudy effect. Leave to dry. As the paint layer is thin, it should be dry within ten minutes or so.

COLOUR WASHING

This technique is similar to the colour rubbing paint finish *(see page 21)*, although in this case the broad brush strokes left by the paintbrush are part of the overall look. The effect is rather rustic in quality and can often be seen on country-style furniture and walls. No glaze is required as the top layer of colour should be very thin and transparent to allow the base to show through the faint wash of colour.

Darker colours work well in this way; applying thinned colours over a paler base coat is often more successful than working with a paler wash over a darker ground. Usually, only a single layer of colour is applied over the base colour and, depending on the effect you require,

the thinned layer of paint can be diluted in a ratio of approximately one part paint to nine parts water. A slightly more opaque wash is created by using one part paint to three parts water, but the effect is not so dramatic. Generally, the thinner the wash, the stronger the top colour needs to be. Small tester pots of colour can be used for the wash: a 0.25 litre (½ pint) can will probably be enough to wash an average-sized room, but do choose the most intense shade you can find. It is unlikely that you will find these stronger colours available off-the-shelf; they are more likely to be mixed to order on a centrifugal colour mixer, so find a paint supplier who can offer this special service, as pastel shades just will not work.

You will need wide paintbrushes for slapping the thinned colour over the base coat. For walls, I suggest you use a very wide 10 cm (4 in) paintbrush or even a 12.5 cm (5 in) (if you can handle it), and plenty of dust sheets (preferably the plastic variety) to protect surfaces that don't require colour washing. For colour washed furniture, use a 7.5 cm (3 in) paintbrush for easier handling. Surfaces can be protected with a layer of matt acrylic varnish, if necessary, to protect the fragile surface. On walls, however, I would leave the colour wash unprotected as a rustic finish should be left to age naturally.

You will find that the wash will dry quickly as you are brushing on diluted emulsion and working it into the surface.

COLOUR WASHING

1 Paint a solid base coat of colour over a prepared and primed surface. You may find you need to apply a second coat, once the first is dry (allow about 30 minutes), to achieve a good, even coverage.

2 Thin the required top colour with water according to the effect you are seeking. For washes applied onto furniture, you may prefer to work with a less diluted top colour. Brush this over the dried base coat.

3 Use a dry paintbrush to spread the top colour over the base coat. Brush outwards in all directions to build up a patchy, uneven layer of colour. The wash should be dry within approximately ten minutes.

DRAGGING

When a long-haired bristle brush is dragged through a wet glaze it leaves behind a subtle, vaguely striped effect which can look effective on pieces of furniture, as well as some wall finishes.

The glaze mix needs to be fairly viscous so that the dragged 'lines' do not blur together. It is useful to set up a test patch on a scrap of old board first before embarking on the real thing. The glaze should also be fairly transparent for the clearest line definition.

Rather than mixing ordinary coloured emulsion paint with acrylic scumble glaze, mix a coloured artist's acrylic colour as this will contain a more intense colour without making the glaze too opaque.

Thin the colour with a little glaze first to amalgamate it, then add this to the rest of the glaze. Brush a little glaze onto a test patch and drag the brush through this: if the glaze holds its ridged surface, then the mixture is perfect; if it is too stiff, it may need a little water. Should the colour be too intense for your requirements, add a teaspoon or so of white emulsion colour to soften it down. Repeat the test procedure again until you are satisfied with the results.

When dragging onto pieces of furniture, work one section at a time, either starting on the top or the legs first. Begin the dragging at a point where there is a vertical to assist your line: for example, at the edge of a table top or against a flat side of a drawer. Brush a layer of the glaze

over the base coat and cover the entire section you are working on. Without delay, start to drag the glaze. It is important to always keep a wet edge to the glaze; never allow the area to be worked to dry out whilst you are working on it. Use the lightest pressure to begin the line of dragging, then increase the pressure on the bristles as you progress down the line. As the line reaches the end, decrease the amount of pressure to finish. Progress in this way until you complete the work.

With walls, it may be simpler to work in a pair so one person applies glaze as the other drags it off.

Glaze slows down the drying rate of water-based acrylic so it is reworkable. Oil glazes take much longer to dry.

DRAGGING

1 Apply two coats of base colour over your prepared surface for a good, even coverage. For dragging on walls, it may be easier to apply paint with a roller. Leave to dry for two to three hours.

2 Mix together the glaze and the top colour and carry out a test patch, as described above, to ensure you have the correct mix and the right balance of colour. Apply the glaze in strips across the surface.

3 Hold the dragging (or long-haired bristle) brush at the top of the glazed section. Apply light pressure at first and carefully pull the brush downwards to form the dragged effect to finish.

COMBING

This is similar to dragging but, rather than pulling a long-haired brush through the still-wet glaze, a fine-toothed rubber comb is used to create the marks. The comb can be pulled straight down to create long, straight rows of glaze or it can be moved from side to side to create a wavy effect. Other patterns may also be created as you wish; a cross-hatched effect or diagonal combing all produce different results. Like dragging, the underlying base colour will show through the glaze so the choice of base colour is just as important as the top glaze.

Special combs can be purchased inexpensively from good decorating stores or art suppliers. If necessary, you could even make your own comb using strong, rigid plastic or a stiff piece of card.

The surface you are decorating should be perfectly smooth for combing. Any lumps or bumps will interrupt the drag of the comb and result in an uneven 'blip' in the glaze. Mix the glaze according to the instructions given for dragging *(see page 23)*. Test the glaze out on a piece of scrap card first and assess once dry as it will alter slightly.

You will need to maintain a steady hand when dragging the comb downwards through the wet glaze. At the start of combing, you will begin working against a door frame or in the corner of a room, where you can use the architrave or wall as a straight edge for the comb. However, as the combing progresses, the only guide for perfectly straight combing is the previously combed marks. Drop a plumb line to help the lines stay vertical and support your combing hand at the elbow with your other hand.

If you wish, an oil-based glaze may be used as opposed to the faster-drying water-based glaze. Mix this in exactly the same way as for the acrylic scumble glaze *(see page 17)*, but tint the glaze with artist's oil colours rather than acrylics or emulsion paints. The oil glaze results in a slightly more hard-wearing surface than the acrylic glazes.

You will notice that, as you end each line, the glaze will have built up around the teeth of the comb. Wipe the excess onto a clean, cotton rag before starting another line.

COMBING

1 Paint the base colour onto your prepared piece of furniture. You will need to brush on two good coats for the best coverage. For an oil-based glaze, use an eggshell paint. Allow four to five hours for drying.

2 Mix up a glaze coat by tinting an oil glaze with artist's oil colours or tinting an emulsion glaze with acrylics. Carry out a test patch on a scrap of board first before committing to the real thing.

3 Whilst the glaze is still wet, pull the teeth of the comb downwards through the glaze, following a wavy or straight line. Clean the comb and repeat. Leave to dry overnight (it will be touch-dry in two to three hours).

ANTIQUING

This technique gives an aged look to the painted surface. It has the appearance of years of wear and tear on a surface, which can look particularly charming in a rustic kind of way *(see page 51)*.

WAX DISTRESSING

There are several ways of achieving the distressed look and the technique described here is perhaps one of the simplest of all, as it uses just paint, abrasive paper and a crucial layer of candle wax.

The choice of emulsion colours is very important. Two colours are characteristically used: one for the base coat and the other for the top coat. When the top coat is rubbed back, the first colour is exposed, so the two colours must work well together. Colours closely related together in tone will create a more subtle and harmonious effect, whereas colours that are opposite in the colour spectrum will be vibrant. Dark green over terracotta red, for instance, would be a dramatic contrast, whereas a creamy yellow over a pale green would create a softer overall effect.

The simulated wear and tear should be heaviest at those places where you would naturally expect the furniture to show most use. Concentrate the block around handles and at the corners of a unit for the best effects. Only one coat of the base colour is required. Rub those areas that are to receive heavy distressing with an ordinary candle.

The wax left behind on the surface of the paint will resist the top layer of paint because oil and water will not mix. In this case, the oil contained in the wax resists the water-based emulsion paint.

The top coat is then brushed on and allowed to dry. Some of the most heavily worked areas may not dry out totally, but this is because of the underlying wax and it will not affect the paint finish. When most of the paint is dry, begin to wear away at the paint layer using abrasive paper. The top layer of paint will easily sand away without too much pressure. Concentrate on sanding those areas that need it most until you are pleased with the general overall effect, making sure all traces of candle wax have been removed.

WAX DISTRESSING

1 Paint a solid colour over the prepared surface and then allow this to dry (about 30 minutes). Using a candle, scrub this over the paint surface to build up a layer of resistance to the next coat of paint.

2 Next paint the second emulsion colour over the wax to cover the base colour completely. Leave this colour to dry (allow about 30 minutes to an hour depending on atmospheric conditions).

3 Carefully rub back the paint layers with a piece of medium-grade abrasive paper to reveal some of the base colour underneath the surface and to produce the desired distressed and antiqued look.

SOFT WAX DISTRESSING

This is another antiquing effect, yet it has a softer, more blurred effect than can be seen in the candle wax method *(see page 25)*. Every technique that uses wax as part of its treatment relies on the principle that oil resists water-based substances. In this way, the soft wax resists the water-based emulsion layer that is applied on top of it. Because the soft wax is applied by brush in a much less precise way than candle wax (which is quite literally drawn onto the paint surface), it makes a softer, distressed finish.

Both the base and top colour are carefully chosen, as they will each be clearly seen in the finished effect. As with most distressed finishes, the combination of colours is the most critical aspect that will determine the overall effect. Stronger colours, such as a cobalt blue worked over a cadmium yellow, will have a striking effect, whereas paler colours will produce a more harmonious finish.

The soft wax that is used could be any one of a number of different furniture waxes, and petroleum jelly also has the same effect although this may be a little stiffer to apply with a brush. Brush the wax onto the dried base coat wherever you need the base coat to show through. Remember that wherever the wax is placed, the top coat of paint will be resisted. Paint a generous coat of the second colour over the wax, taking care not to disturb it too much as the brush is dragged over the top. Allow this to dry. Those areas of paint that are applied over the soft wax will tend to stay quite wet, but this is perfectly normal. When the paint in other areas is quite dry, you can then start to wipe away the top colour. You will notice that the wax comes away too, and it is important to remove all of this from the surface. A soft cloth should remove all the wax and the damp, overlying colour. Some wax will be absorbed into the surrounding matt paint, which has the combined effect of producing a silky, soft finish, which forms a protective barrier. A soft wax distressed effect is less defined than one with harder candle wax and the two colours become blurred at the edges. I have had good results with an off-white creamy top coat over a pale oatmeal beige base.

SOFT WAX DISTRESSING

1 Paint the base colour over a prepared surface and allow this to dry (about 30 minutes to an hour). Using a soft cloth (a dry dishcloth is perfect), apply the soft wax in broad patches all over the surface.

2 When the base coat is dry, paint the second layer of emulsion colour over the wax, taking care not to brush the wax out too much. Be generous with the paint, as lots of this will be removed later on.

3 When the second colour has dried on those areas where there is no wax (about 30 minutes to an hour), wipe the surface firmly with a dry cloth. This will remove wax and paint to reveal a softly distressed effect.

TWO-COLOUR ANTIQUING WITH WAX

Throughout the whole of this book, I depend largely upon a handful of paint effects. Some are built up with layers of transparent washes of paint, such as colour washing; others are aided by adding transparent acrylic scumble glaze to create softer layers of colour, and some are formed simply by distressing one colour to reveal an underlying one. A finish referred to as 'antiquing' is seeing an enormous popularity at the moment and it is an effect I use frequently throughout this book.

There are a number of techniques used to produce an antique look but, and more often than not, the look is produced when a dark-coloured beeswax is applied over the top layer of colour. The antique effect can be administered over a surface that already has a paint effect upon it, but once the wax is applied no other treatment can be carried out as the wax will resist everything other than itself. In two-colour distressing, two colours are applied roughly over each other and allowed to dry. The colours painted onto the surface will vary a little once the coloured wax is rubbed over the top due to stainers in the wax. There are lots of variations in the colour of these waxes, and so it may be an idea to experiment on a piece of scrap card first before committing yourself to the real thing.

To achieve a more distressed finish, wax is applied with a pad of wire wool which literally 'scrubs' the wax into the surface of the paint. To create a softer application which does not disturb the underlying paint, apply the wax with a soft, lint-free cotton cloth.

The wax gives the painted surface a silky-smooth finish, which will be resistant to knocks and scrapes, and provides a wipe-clean surface. You will find that the colours used for this effect look particularly good if the tones are close. A favourite combination of mine is a greeny-toned off-white emulsion with a sage green emulsion *(see the tray on pages 52–53)*, combined with a heavy distress of wax applied with abrasive wire wool. The final result is subtle and restrained, rather like the finish that can be seen on painted antique Swedish furniture.

TWO-COLOUR ANTIQUING WITH WAX

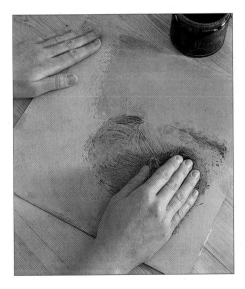

1 Paint your first colour over a prepared background. This can be roughly applied in a rather patchy fashion. Brush the paint outwards so that it spreads in all directions, but keep the paint thickness fairly even.

2 After 30 minutes to an hour, apply the second layer of colour, filling in any remaining spaces. None of the primer should be visible through the painted layers. Leave to dry for 30 minutes to an hour.

3 Load a pad of medium-grade wire wool with a tinted furniture wax. Scrub this into the paint surface to incorporate it into the surface and to remove some underlying paint. Buff with a dry cloth.

CRACKLE GLAZE

Here is another antiquing effect that simulates years of age upon a painted surface. You may often notice that the top layer of paint on old painted walls and skirting boards has started to peel and crack. This effect is easily recreated with an inexpensive crackle medium that is brushed between two coats of emulsion paint.

Crackle medium is available from good decorating suppliers or art and craft stores. It is brushed on fairly thinly, so a little can go a long way. For the crackle glaze to work, you will always need to use water-based paints. Choose matt emulsion paints whenever possible as some vinyl paints, although water-based, can have too much of a plastic-like quality, which makes the crackle less effective. If in doubt, carry out a small test patch first. The effect is particularly dramatic if strongly contrasting colours are used – a rich crimson red, for example, under duck egg blue. If the colours are closer in tone, a subdued look is achieved and the effect of the crackle is then far less noticeable.

The crackle medium is applied once the base coat is completely dry (about 30 minutes to an hour). It should be applied over the surface, with the brush strokes following the same direction. Only when the varnish is totally dry should the second layer of emulsion be applied. Almost as soon as you start to apply the top layer you will see the crackle glaze starting to take effect. You will need to work quite quickly. It is impor-tant not to go over any parts of the freshly applied paint as the surface is rather fragile whilst peeling is taking place. Any bits that are missed can be touched in later once the top coat has dried.

When dry (allow about an hour), the item can be coated in clear varnish for protection. For this, use a spirit-based polyurethane varnish. Smaller items, such as picture and mirror frames, hat boxes or bedside tables, look good with some or all of their surfaces treated in this way, but avoid treating larger items as the effect can be too much. On a larger cupboard or door, for example, it may be more effective to crackle glaze only a part of the unit, such as between any panelling or around the sides, to define important details.

CRACKLE GLAZE

1 Paint a layer of the base coat over the prepared background. If you notice any lumps on the surface, sand these with abrasive paper first to obtain the smoothest possible base, as they may spoil the finished effect.

2 When the paint is totally dry (allow about 30 minutes to an hour), apply a thin layer of the transparent crackle medium. Apply this carefully to some or all parts of the item to be crackled.

3 Allow the crackle medium to dry (about 30 minutes to an hour), then apply the second emulsion layer. Apply the wet paint in one direction only. Charge the brush fully and work quickly. Leave to dry as before.

CRACKLE GLAZE WITH ANTIQUING WAX

This finish uses crackle glaze, but rather than finishing with a layer of varnish, antique wax is rubbed into the peeled paint. The wax seals and protects the surface but, rather more importantly, it adds a depth of colour that enriches the paint colour and lends an antiqued appearance.

Follow the same procedure as outlined for crackle glaze *(see page 28)*. The same colour rules apply to this particular technique as for the more regular finishes and these are principally that colours that are clearly sympathetic in tone produce a greater effect of harmony, whereas colours that are opposites in the spectrum achieve more dramatic finishes. Once the peeled paint is completely dry, the wax is applied. Again, for a more dramatic effect, the wax is applied with a pad of wire wool, which has the combined effect of both pushing the paint deep into the open cracks of the top layer and removing paint at the same time to further accentuate the distressed nature of the finish.

To produce a good crackle effect, it is important to brush the glaze out very thinly across the dry base coat. As the top coat reacts with the crackle glaze, the whole surface becomes quite fragile. This can be difficult to control on a vertical surface. In the past I have occasionally seen the whole top coat literally slide right off a piece of furniture. Bearing this mistake clearly in mind then, it is far easier to work on a horizontal surface. For furniture and three-dimensional objects, first work on one side of your piece of furniture. Allow this to dry (about an hour), then work on another side and so on until the piece is completed. It may be more time-consuming, but it is worth it in the long run.

If you have difficulty obtaining crackle glaze, you can make up your own medium using gum arabic. Gum arabic crystals (or liquid) are dissolved in a little boiling water to make up a sticky, viscous glaze. This is then used in the same way as the regular, commercially purchased glaze, although you may need to apply two or three layers in order to build up a good glaze coat. Test the effect on a piece of scrap paper first before beginning.

CRACKLE GLAZE WITH ANTIQUING WAX

1 Paint the base colour onto the prepared ground, maintaining a good, even coverage. When this is completely dry (30 minutes to an hour), brush on a layer of crackle glaze and leave this to dry as before.

2 Apply the second layer of emulsion once the glaze is dry. Use a loaded brush and work quickly, as the surface cannot be reworked, applying the paint in one direction only until the glaze is covered.

3 When all the layers are dry (allow approximately an hour), rub antiquing wax into the peeled paint surface to finish the effect. Use a circular movement with the pad to push paint deeply into the cracks.

CRACKLE VARNISH

Like the peeling paint effect of crackle glaze *(see pages 28–29)*, here is another technique that simulates an old, cracked varnished surface. In this case the technique uses two varnishes, one applied over the other, but both have different drying times. Usually the varnishes have different solvents, one is oil-based and the other one is water-based. However, all of these two-part varnishes are different; they rely on the two-part system, but some have two types of water-based varnishes. Always check the manufacturer's instructions prior to their use.

As both varnishes react together on the painted surface, a network of tiny cracks will appear, reminiscent of the crackled varnish seen on many old paintings. The effect is much softer than the crackle glaze technique. Because the cracks on this surface are so fine, it is common to rub a little burnt umber artist's oil colour over the dry surface of the varnish to highlight the fine crackles. Once the base coat is dry and any surface decoration has been applied, the first part of the two-stage process is applied. The first coat of varnish is thinly brushed out over the surface. A regular household paintbrush is used to apply the varnish. If you are thinking of using this technique more often, it may be a worthwhile investment to buy specialist varnish brushes for this particular use as you are more able to control the amount of varnish you are using with one of these brushes.

Once the first coat is touch-dry (but still tacky when pressed), it is ready for the second stage. This second application of varnish dries much quicker than the first and, in about half an hour, you should start to see the tiny cracks appearing. You may need to hold the object up to a light source as the cracks are often so fine. When the second layer is dry, use a soft cotton cloth and rub a small amount of brown oil colour all over the surface. The oil colour is held in the tiny cracks and the cracks are then clearly seen.

When the oil paint has dried (in four to five hours for touch-drying), the crackled surface should then be sealed with a layer of polyurethane varnish for further protection. Leave overnight to dry.

CRACKLE VARNISH

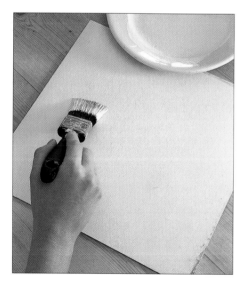  

1 Apply a base colour over the prepared surface and brush it out well. Apply two coats, if necessary. Allow the first coat to dry completely (about 30 minutes to an hour) before applying the second.

2 Thinly apply a layer of the first varnish over the dried emulsion. Brush the varnish outwards in all directions to maintain a thin, even layer. When tacky, apply the second varnish in the same way.

3 When the varnishes are dry (in about two to three hours) and you can see a fine network of cracks over the surface, use a cotton cloth to rub artist's oil colour over the surface to highlight the cracks.

LINING

This is a very simple way of adding an elegant touch to a fairly plain, surface *(see also page 57)*. The lines are drawn in by hand first using chalk or a soft, coloured crayon and they are then filled in with a long-haired artist's brush. Long-haired lining brushes are available commercially, but these can be expensive and you need practice. The longer-haired brushes, available from artists' brush ranges, will be perfectly adequate for the projects outlined in this book.

Guide lines are drawn over the prepared surface using either a long ruler or a piece of timber that will act as a long, straight edge. Mark the position of the line on the surface using a ruler, then simply join these marks together with the ruler or timber. Thin a little of your chosen lining colour with the appropriate solvent (oil-based colour is thinned with white spirit and water-based colours need water), so that the paint is thin enough to flow easily along the marked line, but opaque enough to register over the base colour. You may find that it is easier to practise on a piece of scrap paper before starting on the real thing. Artists' oil or acrylic colours are the best products to use for lining as the colours can be thinned easily, yet they still retain their intensity.

You will find it easier to paint if your hand is supported along the edge of the surface on which you are working. While maintaining a steady hand position, one finger supported on the edge of the table or object that is being painted, place the loaded brush in position and drag your brush down the edge of the line, keeping it steady. Guide your brush slowly along the line. To retrace your steps once a brush is reloaded, pull the brush along the original line following exactly the same path, then adopt the same hand position and increase the pressure on the brush each time you start to create a new part of the lining. Aim to exert the same pressure on the brush as before as this will determine the thickness of the line.

If you then wish to create a thicker line, do not be tempted to simply choose a fatter-bristled brush as opposed to a lining brush as you will find that this will be more difficult to control.

LINING

1 Mark out the positions of the lining using a ruler and a piece of chalk or crayon. Join the marks together to produce the guide lines for the lining brush to follow. Draw in decorative corners, if required.

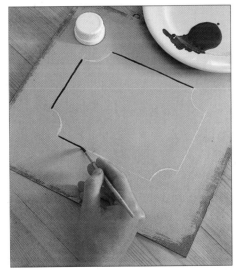

2 Use a narrow artist's brush to paint in the fine lining. The longer-haired brushes will hold more paint than shorter-haired ones and are easier to use. Leave gaps at the corners for the decorative details.

3 Paint in the decorative corners last of all. Keep a steady hand and maintain an even pressure on the brush. To achieve a neat and thicker line, paint in two parallel lines and then fill in the gap between them.

GETTING STARTED

Over the next few pages you will find all the basic know-how you need to get yourself going and (hopefully) to produce some fantastic pieces of furniture and fabulous effects around your home. The first thing to consider is where to start and which stamp to use, and the projects and items stamped in this book will, I trust, give you some guidance. From trinket boxes to tables, picture frames, planters and porcelain, I hope that we've covered just about everything you will ever need to know about decorating around your home with stamps. In the techniques pages that follow you will learn how to make up your own blocks and there are guidelines for stamping a huge range of materials. From here onwards, you'll find all the information you need to produce wonderful effects – it's just a case of starting.

STAMP DESIGNS

Once you have decided on the type of look you would like and chosen from the many designs outlined at the back of this book, trace the design onto a piece of white paper. Decide whether you will need to enlarge or reduce this design. It is often easiest for a complete beginner to choose a smaller design at first, as the block is simpler to control.

When you have an outline that is the right size, trim away the excess. Use a small amount of spray adhesive to provide a 'just tacky' surface to secure the paper outline onto the piece of rubber. Spray outdoors if possible or fold a piece of paper around three sides of the work (sealed with masking tape) to contain the spray. If you apply too much you will find it difficult to peel the paper off the rubber once the outline has been cut. Use a small pair of

MAKING A STAMP

  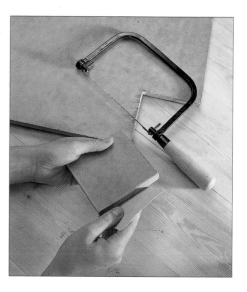

1 Trace off the motif you wish to use and transfer the design onto ordinary writing paper. If you want to reduce or enlarge the pattern, use a photocopier until your design is the correct scale for your chosen project.

2 Use a small amount of spray adhesive to tack the design onto the rubber surface, then cut it out with a small pair of scissors. You may need to use a sharp craft knife for more intricate pieces.

3 Cut a printing block from an offcut of wood or MDF. The block must be thick enough for you to grip it at the sides with your fingertips. Smooth any rough edges away with abrasive paper.

sharp scissors or a craft knife to cut all around the outline. A scalpel may also be used on a cutting mat, but be careful of the extremely sharp blade. Soft foam rubber can be cut very easily. However, care should be taken, particularly when cutting intricate parts of a design. Hold the cutting edge of the scalpel at a right angle to the rubber and make sure you cut away from yourself.

PREPARING THE BLOCK

The more square your sawn piece of timber, the easier printing will be. Use a metal right angle to mark out the square perfectly and score the lines in dark pencil. The size of your block is determined by the size of image. Use a ruler to measure both the length and width of the image accurately – it may be either square or rectangular. The image should fit neatly inside the block, with the edges of the design just touching but not overlapping the sides.

I tend to use thick MDF (medium-density fibreboard) for stamping blocks as it is strong, easy to cut and does not warp. However, almost any material could be used, providing it is easy to saw and thick enough to hold between your fingertips at the sides. Look for offcuts in your local DIY store. Cut the block using a fretsaw or power saw, if you have one. Always align the cutting edge of the saw with the marked lines. Smooth down any rough edges using fine-grade abrasive paper to create a perfect block that is now ready for the foam rubber to be applied.

MAKING THE BLOCK

It is important that you transfer the drawn image of the design onto both sides of the block. Primarily, it is outlined onto the front to ensure that the foam rubber pieces are perfectly aligned. You will find it is extremely useful to have the perfect mirror image of the stamp facing you on the reverse side of the block, as this will help you greatly when you are later positioning the block onto your chosen surface.

Always use contact adhesive to secure the rubber pieces onto the block. Do not be tempted to use any other kind of adhesive as it may either deteriorate the rubber or else it may not provide a strong enough bond to hold the rubber pieces in position on the block.

4 Before you stick the rubber pieces down, trace the outline of the design onto both the front and back of the block. Ensure that both outlines are identically placed for accurate positioning of the block.

5 Apply contact adhesive to both the foam rubber and block to bond them together. Use a small piece of card to spread this evenly over the block and larger motif pieces. Allow to dry until tacky (about 30 minutes).

6 Once the contact adhesive is dry, pick up each rubber section and position carefully on the block, using the outline as a guide. You can use tweezers to handle the smaller pieces. Your block is now ready for printing.

DESIGNING YOUR OWN STAMPS

It's not difficult to make up your own stamps, either from your own drawings or directly from an outline that you have copied from elsewhere. Foam rubber can be cut into practically any shape you want, from fine-lined motifs to bold graphic designs.

The most important tool that you will need is a sharp scalpel or craft knife. Tracing paper and a soft pencil will also be needed if you want to copy your design from another source (such as a real leaf, as featured below) or from an inspiring book or magazine.

MAKING A MOTIF

To make up your own stamp motif, you will need to select your source material. In the photograph opposite, a straightforward leaf shape is drawn onto tracing paper following the outline of a real fallen leaf. The same technique may be used to draw around a single flower or a flattish shell – a scallop would be perfect. Simple shapes often work really well and, for those who may be more artistically challenged, this is a great way of obtaining some quite unique original source material.

Pat the leaf with some kitchen paper towel to blot any moisture before sliding it under a sheet of tracing paper. Flatten it slightly and draw around the outside of each part. If mistakes are made, then outlines are easily erased using a pencil eraser. Use a small amount of spray mount to tack the tracing paper over the foam rubber surface (position the tracing paper over the corner of the foam sheet to minimize the amount of waste foam). Cut out the shape using a sharp craft knife on a cutting mat, following the drawn lines as carefully as possible.

Don't worry if parts of the design are separate from each other as the motif will be reassembled later. Taking the leaf opposite as an example, each of the separate components were cut out separately, as was the central stalk. All the pieces were then put together on the block.

MAKING A LEAF STAMP

A real leaf is blotted dry and then placed underneath a semi-transparent sheet of tracing paper and the outline is traced off using a pencil. The traced motif is then positioned over the foam rubber and the parts are cut out using a sharp craft knife then assembled onto a printing block and glued in position with contact adhesive. Once this is thoroughly dry, the motif is then ready for stamping.

STAMPING ONTO WALLS

Stamping onto walls is easy, effective and it can be surprisingly great fun *(see pages 62–65)*. It often has a similar effect to a stencil, but it is much easier to do and, unlike stencilling, you don't need to follow a complicated registering procedure.

The overall finished effect is really up to you. If a richly patterned all-over design, rather like the effect of an expensive hand-blocked wallpaper, appeals to you then the stamp is worked over a tight grid. If an open effect is more to your liking, then the same motif can be worked over the walls, but on a larger grid system. Other, and equally effective, alternatives could be to use more than one stamp design across a wall area. You will find that the possibilities for stamping are quite endless.

MAKING A GRID

The process of making a grid is much simpler than it may at first sound. For a densely patterned surface, you will need to cut a square card former that is approximately 25 cm (10 in) square. Experiment with the size of the square to achieve your desired effect: basically, the smaller the size of your square, the more compact your design will be, i.e. the closer the stamps will be to each other. For a much more random spacing of the stamped motif, cut a card former that is at least 45 cm (18 in) square.

Drop a plumb line from the ceiling and wait until the weighted bob lies flat against the wall (secure this to the ceiling with a thumb tack or a piece of masking tape). Hold the former diagonally behind the plumb line so that the line crosses through the middle of both the top and bottom corners of the square. Use white chalk to mark each of the four corners of the square with a small cross. Slide the card across to line up the two sides of the card with two more chalk marks, and then mark the two remaining corners with a chalk cross. Continue working in this way, moving right across the wall, until the whole area is marked up with a range of small chalked crosses. Each stamp is then positioned centrally over each cross to build up a regular printed pattern.

PREPARATION

If your walls already have a freshly painted surface, you may be able to start stamping directly onto them. However, for those who may perhaps have inherited rather less attractive walls, some considerable time may need to be spent on preparation before any stamping can take place.

Wipe down existing paintwork with a soft cloth and warm, soapy water and then assess the situation. If the colour looks tired or is perhaps just a little too 'flat', then a quick and easy colour wash *(see page 22)* may be all that is required to give a lift. If you have walls that are deeply cracked and pitted, then the surface may need to be filled, sanded and sealed first. Carry out these repairs and apply a base coat over the raw filler. You may need to base-coat the whole room depending on the extent of the repairs. Both of these scenarios are preferable to being faced with textured wallpaper or (and even worse) a woodchip wallpaper, which are both sadly ubiquitous in many homes. If your room is of average size and it is covered in either of these papers, then I recommend that you strip away these offensive types of wall covering, preferably with a steam stripper. These can be hired from DIY stores. If you are presented with a larger than average-sized room, covered with either woodchip or textured paper, you will just have to grit your teeth seriously and get on with it. As a compromise, a flat colour or a colour wash paint effect *(see page 22)* could be brushed over woodchip wall paper and then, when dry, it could be stamped. If the task is too daunting or if, perhaps more importantly, you suspect that the woodchip is, in fact, holding the walls together, then it is undoubtedly more preferable to live with stamped woodchip walls than a pile of rubble!

PAINT

With wall finishes, the best surface on which to stamp (and to use for stamping) is matt emulsion paint. Avoid vinyl ranges as these have a slippery and silky finish that makes your carefully positioned stamp slide off the wall once any pressure is exerted upon it. If your walls are painted with a vinyl paint on a poor surface, you have little choice but to sand down and repaint the walls. To load the stamp, pour paint into a tray or saucer and press the block into it. Coat the block evenly with a layer of paint and position it carefully on the surface. Apply an equal pressure over the block to transfer the paint. Lift it cleanly away. If any mistakes should occur, wipe these away from the wall immediately using a cloth dampened with water, dry and repeat your stamp.

SPECIAL EFFECTS

A variety of different finishes can be achieved with the stamping block itself to add even more character to the effect. Whether you are working on smaller furniture items or over larger wall areas, any of these special effects can be incorporated either onto isolated stamps or with all the stamped motifs. Small hand-painted flourishes can be quickly dashed in to break up the regularity of a repeating stamp. A three-dimensional effect may be used along a stamped border for a dado. Or the printed stamp can be given a distressed look to complement a rustic effect. Exerting uneven pressure on the block produces shadows on the printed motif and this works well when a more hand-painted effect is required.

STAMPING WITH UNEVEN PRESSURE

This special effect relies on an uneven pressure being exerted upon the back of the printing block. Rather than pressing evenly over the whole surface, position the block then use the fingertips to exert pressure, on the right- or left-hand side of the stamping block. This technique can be worked in a number of different ways: firstly, pressure may be applied to the same side of each stamp every time a motif is about to be printed. Secondly, the pressure may be altered randomly for each motif: first from the right and then from the left side, then either the top or the very bottom of the printing block. Alternatively, uneven printing may be used on only a few of the stamped motifs to introduce some sort of a 'break' in a more regular, repeating style of pattern. I have found that this effect is particularly successful when it is used on pieces of smaller furniture.

STAMPING WITH UNEVEN PRESSURE

1 Brush a little colour onto a flat surface and then press your stamping block evenly into the paint. Lift the block away from the paint and check that the paint has transferred successfully.

2 Position the stamp onto the surface, using chalk registration marks for correct alignment if necessary. Press on one side of the stamping block, taking care not to let the block slide.

3 Lift off the block to reveal the stamped image. The aim is to achieve a more strongly printed edge on the side where most pressure was exerted and a faintly-printed effect on the opposite side.

DISTRESSING THE STAMP

This technique 'knocks back' a neatly transferred stamp motif into its underlying base colour to give an attractive aged effect. Abrasive wire wool or abrasive paper is used to 'scrub' the surface of the printed stamp to literally wear it away. The amount of wearing away depends on the object on which you are working. Heavily rusticated pieces benefit from a heavy-handed approach, where the resulting stamped image just ghosts through. Some stamps, on the other hand, only require a restrained amount of wear and tear to simply 'knock back' the freshness of a stamp in order to help it appear slightly aged and fashionably worn.

This effect is nearly always very successful when used on either a colour washed or antiqued background (see pages 22 and 25–30) as this helps to accentuate the aged quality that is so desirable.

The technique works particularly well inside the panels of a cupboard door: for example, when the outside of the cabinet features an antiqued crackle glaze paint effect (see page 29). Or over a two-colour distressed paint effect (see page 25).

The great thing about this effect is that you need never worry about achieving the perfect print every time. In fact, the more uneven the print is the better, as this quality lends a particular charm to a piece. Some stamps may be printed twice before you stop to reload.

Use emulsion paints for the stamping, if possible, as these are easier to distress. Artists' colours tend to have more of a saturated colour and can stain the underlying base colours, and they are difficult to obliterate to near extinction, if that's the look that is required. The stamping effect leaves a slightly pitted texture on the surface of each stamped motif, giving the abrasive paper or wire wool something to grip onto and making the surface easier to distress.

For much larger surfaces, you may prefer to use a power sander to achieve faster results. Use a fine-grade abrasive paper and wear away at the stamped area by degrees. Check the results as you go along to control the amount of distressing. On smaller areas, however, I would recommend the hand method.

DISTRESSING THE STAMP

1 Load the block in the usual way and print the stamp motif over your prepared surface. Remove the block and repeat until the whole area to be stamped is completed. Allow to dry (about 30 minutes).

2 Use a pad of medium-grade wire wool or abrasive paper to wear away at the stamp. Work in a circular motion and check the amount of distressing regularly to achieve the perfect finish.

3 Finally, repeat exactly the same procedure on all the stamps. Furniture may then be waxed or varnished for protection. Walls can be left untreated or finished with a layer of matt acrylic varnish.

STAMPING TO CREATE A SHADOW

This effect gives a three-dimensional quality to a stamped image. The shadow is created whenever a paler-coloured stamp is printed over a darker, ink-coloured stamp. It is most important to always remember to mark the printing position of the first block so that the second stamp can be moved either slightly to the left or right of this first position. Ordinary white chalk or a soft pencil should be used as this can be easily wiped or erased away when the finished stamp is dry.

The second stamping colour needs to be fairly opaque so that it can cover the underlying darker colour. Opaque paints invariably mean the kind that contain lots of white pigment in the paint mix. A cost effective way of ensuring the right colour, together with the right amount of opacity, would be to mix up your own shade using a matt white emulsion paint with artists' acrylic colours. Tint the white with acrylic colour until the perfect balance is reached. You will find that it is easier to test the stamping colours on a piece of scrap card before committing yourself to the real thing.

To mark up the block, first load your stamp, using the first colour, in the usual way. Position the block over the surface and lower, then press down before lifting off. Lightly mark in the four corners of the block with a piece of chalk. Lift off the block and continue in the same way, aligning the stamp with the corner marks as you go along, until the first colour stamps have all been applied onto the surface. Rinse the block under cool water and pat dry to remove any excess water. Then reload the stamp with the second colour. Hold the block over the registration marks and move it slightly to one side, lower and press the back of the block to transfer the paint. Lift the block off to reveal the shadow effect. Repeat as required. When all the stamps are thoroughly dry, rub off the registration marks. Try to ensure that the distance between the two stamps is more or less equal each time to make sure the stamps are roughly the same. Judge this by eye or move the block (say the width of a finger each time) to maintain a certain regularity of pattern.

STAMPING TO CREATE A SHADOW

1 Load the first block with a dark, inky colour in the usual way, and carefully position this over the prepared surface. Press the block firmly down on the surface, exerting an even pressure on the back.

2 Lightly mark the corners of the block with white chalk or a soft pencil before carefully lifting it away from the surface. Allow the first colour to dry completely (this should take approximately 30 minutes).

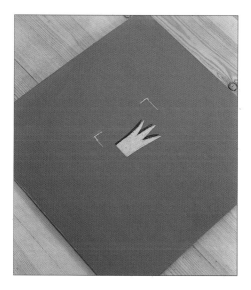

3 Rinse and dry the block, then load with the second colour. Use the chalk marks to position the block. Move it slightly to one side, lower and then press down. Lift the block away to reveal the stamp.

STAMPING WITH HAND-FINISHED DETAIL

Regardless of size, hand-painted flourishes add another dimension to a stamped surface. It need not be a grand gesture by any means: a small wispy line, dashed in to represent a stalk on a leaf, for example, will be enough. Small berries, painted below a couple of holly leaves or a wavy line under a seashell, can all be simply painted in as details at the end of the stamping process.

The good thing about adding in a hand-painted line, spot, dash (or whatever) is that nothing needs to be precise. Unlike the regular print of each stamp, the hand-painted detail can vary from one to the other; stalks on a leaf can first go in one direction and then in the other.

Generally, in most cases, I would always add the hand-painted details onto the surface once the stamping is finished and it has thoroughly dried. This particular effect works especially well used over larger areas of stamping: on walls or larger pieces of furniture. The hand-painted irregular lines break up the graphic sharpness of a large stamped area and trick the eye into breaking up the regular pattern.

A variety of paint finishes can further enforce this deception. Metallic paints work well as a strong contrast between the shiny, glittery surface of the paint and the flat matt quality of the emulsion. Artists' acrylic colours feature some very good metallic colours, which are easy to apply and to work with, and they

also have the added benefit of being completely washable in water, so any spills, drips or splodges can be easily wiped away.

To prevent any mistakes, you may find it is an advantage to draw in the proposed flourishes with chalk before committing yourself to the real thing. In this way, you can see how the final effect will look. If the look is too heavy, the chalk lines can be easily wiped away with a damp cloth and the area can be worked upon again and again until the balance is correct.

Paint the detail in alongside the chalk line then, when the paint is dry, you can wipe the chalk mark clean away. Hand-painted lines can first be measured by eye, then dashed in with a confident brush stroke.

STAMPING WITH HAND-FINISHED DETAIL

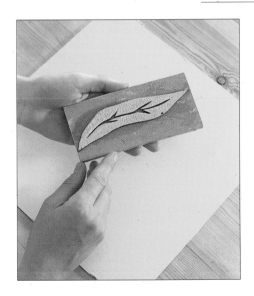

1 Load your stamp in the usual way and position it over the surface. If you are placing the block over a fixed point, you will need to align this very carefully with the centre of the stamp.

2 Press the block onto the surface taking care not to let the block slide. Try to work on a flat, horizontal surface if possible. When stamping onto walls, you may find it easier to work with a partner.

3 When the printed stamp is dry, add in a simple hand-painted flourish using a fine artist's brush. This could be anything from the stalk shown here to a shadow effect painted over a floral motif.

COLOUR SCHEMES

Colours flavour our lives in a most powerful and evocative way. Strong reds and oranges are passionate colours, whereas cool blues and greens can be calming and restful. Every colour has its own effect upon us and we tend to know what we do or do not like, particularly for our homes. Here we explore two colour combinations that are strong and influential in the world of decorating at this moment in time.

They are the neutrals, which are often earth colours (and many of these are derived from naturally occurring materials), and we also explore the stronger 'spicy' palette of colours dominated by richer shades. Both colour schemes are used a great deal by decorators and designers alike and, perhaps more excitingly, at the moment, stronger colours are beginning to supersede sales of white and white with hints of colour.

NEUTRALS

Inspiration comes from diverse sources: limestone tiles that have been quarried from deep earth resources, to decorative seed balls that are constructed from a handful of tiny haricots. The neutral palette is all around us, in shells and pebbles from a child's collection, and in the simply-styled fabrics and towels from a high street store.

The range of neutrals is vast. Certainly, it far exceeds the limited palette of cream magnolia or white, and the new neutrals greatly surpass any shade of brown. Linen, calico, raffia and stone are great starting points from which we can explore the whole diversity of this wonderful palette of colours. Ammonite fossils or pebbles, picked from the beach, all display their glorious colours, alongside rope, twigs, shells and string.

LOOKING AT COLOURS

Choosing the right colour can be daunting, but you will find it much easier if you immerse yourself in paint charts, fabrics, magazines and anything else that gives you an exciting range of styles and ideas. Literally surround yourself with spread charts and articles on a table top in front of you and just look. What colours appeal to you most? Perhaps you may favour the cooler shades, or maybe the warmer ones? Generally, people naturally gravitate towards their favourite colours. If selection is still tricky, start to remove those colours that you like least and then look at those that are left. Are the remaining colours all linked in some way, and do they have a common characteristic? Do not automatically despair if you already

NEUTRALS

An important consideration when dealing with a neutral colour scheme is to avoid using too much of any one colour. A monochrome effect would be dull and lifeless, lacking any energy. On the other hand, a well-chosen scheme is one that uses a variety of colours and textures. Colours are layered over one another and combine well together to build up a rich effect. Natural raffia and the soft beiges and creams of pebbles all illustrate the enormous variety of neutrals that are available.

have both blue and red colours together: some blues have lots of warm magenta tones in them and so these can be warm blues. Study the shades carefully and form your choice of colour scheme based on those colours that are still on the table in front of you.

CHOOSING A COLOUR SCHEME

Select lots of objects, fabrics or fruits (whatever you have around your home) and spread these out together in front of you, either across the floor or over a table top. Look at it all closely and reject anything that you may feel that you could never live with, for whatever reason. Perhaps a certain pink reminds you of old ladies' clothes? It doesn't matter – reject it! Soon you'll have built up a collection of colours that you really do like.

Using your favourite colours in a room scheme can be very bold and sometimes daunting too. If you've carried out the selection procedure outlined here, you may be left with a deep purple as your most favourite colour. Well, some of us could live with deeper shades but to others, well, quite honestly you'd have to forget it! It's all very well making a jump from magnolia walls to those with just a hint of colour, but it takes a brave person to immediately start to brush deep purple over the spare room. An important consideration is not to select a single colour scheme, but to look at colours in relation to others. Monochromatic schemes are just as applicable with bold colours as they are when using the neutral palette. Too much of one colour can be heavy, dull and lifeless. Think about introducing different textures, such as fabric or glass, stone, wood or marble. Allow one colour to dominate (and this will inevitably be the wall colour) and balance the other colours around this. Subtle touches of one colour can create a strong visual impact and accentuate other colours around it.

When you start to decorate, the wall colour will undoubtedly appear to be strong and may be overpowering, as it is unlikely that any of the furniture is in the room while you are painting. Be brave and do not be deterred; be confident in your choice of colour regardless of how different it looks on the walls, as opposed to the colour in the tin or even on the paint chart. Colours are affected by the pictures you hang on the walls and the curtains you hang at the windows. Any number of variables will alter the wall colour once they are introduced into the room.

Work on a small test area first before committing yourself to the whole room. Many paint companies will supply small tester pots of colour. Use these colours on a scrap of board or an area of wall that isn't immediately visible (behind a sofa or door, perhaps). View the colours at different times of day and see how the light affects them. And make sure you choose an appropriate time of day for viewing the colour in accordance with when the room will actually be used.

A RICH PALETTE OF COLOURS

The inspiration for these glorious colours is drawn from a number of very different sources: rich purples and plums, magentas and deep burgundies are all exquisite examples of these rich shades. Think of ripe fruit and printed and woven fabrics from hotter climates. Vermilion, cadmium red and alizarin crimson are all deeply evocative colours that may be successfully combined to create many interesting and varied effects around our homes.

Part Two
PROJECTS

This part of the book looks closely at five separate rooms in a typical home – the kitchen, living room, bedroom, bathroom and nursery. Each room has its own specific requirements for decoration – a table and chairs in the kitchen or a mirror frame in the bathroom, whatever. You'll also find that every room has its own set of stamps that are relevant to its particular style, and the detailed step-by-step sequences demonstrate clearly how to progress your stamping technique. Bold treatments are explored for a colonial-style living room and romantic decorations are used for a bedroom. Other influences for different rooms in the house are inspired by spiralling shapes, Scandinavian furniture and the classic fleur de lys motif, amongst many others.

The
KITCHEN

*S*oft, dappled walls in warm, sunny shades reflect the light and create the perfect backdrop for this simple country-style kitchen. Whether it is in the heart of the city or the depths of the countryside, this style is appealing to practically everyone and evokes a kind of nostalgia for everything that is simply designed, uncomplicated and yet highly efficient at the same time.

The kitchen often doubles up as a place for many other activities and is not solely for cooking or eating. Yes, it is a place to entertain, but it can also be used for reading the newspaper, potting plants, sewing, writing and painting – any number of pastimes and pleasures that we all seek to undertake. It is a place that stimulates us to fulfil all of these things if we wish to, or simply to sit, think and then wait to be inspired.

Whether you're making over old junk furniture, creating accessories from scratch or revamping existing kitchen items, you should find a solution to your kitchen problems in this chapter. And don't underestimate the usefulness of old junk items – both the wall cupboard and the base units used in the projects that follow were uncovered in dusty old junk shops and given a new lease of life.

A RUSTIC WALL CUPBOARD

MATERIALS: *Old paintbrush, paint stripper, stripping knife, masking tape, Stanley knife, soft cloths, vinegar, household paintbrush, acrylic primer, base and top coat emulsions (off-white and yellow ochre), paint kettle, crackle glaze, 7.5 cm (3in) paintbrush, antiquing wax, tape measure, chalk or pencil, floral and leaf motif stamps (see pages 119 and 123), deep pink and dark blue emulsion, plate, acrylic varnish, screw fixings and replacement handles.*

Junk furniture is ideal for stamping and I was lucky enough to find this beautifully proportioned cupboard in my local junk store. The cupboard was heavily coated in thick brown stainers and varnish, and so it would have been a really time-consuming task to strip all the old layers away. After a little haggling, I was able to get the cupboard for a good price with that all-important delivery charge thrown in. You will need an extra pair of hands when tackling a big project like this, and this cupboard was extremely heavy.

As a great fan of painted furniture, I had already decided on the fate of this cupboard. The antiqued, rather rustic style of decorating certainly seems to

have taken a hold of many decorators' plans at the moment and this cupboard was about to follow that course, which was a far cry from its original state.

Although the cupboard would have been suited to almost any room in the house, I decorated it for use in the kitchen. This room has a relaxed country style and generally has an informal feeling about it. The base colours I chose for the cupboard are soft, harmonious shades to complement each other, rather than contrasting colours. These colours were in contrast to the heavy, dark wood from which the cupboard was made, and lighten the whole look. A yellow ochre underlies an off-white emulsion paint and a layer of crackle glaze *(see pages 28–29)* between the two colours splits the paint to give an instantly ageing effect. The unique character of old, peeling paint is quickly achieved. Once the top colour is applied over the dried glaze, the paint starts to 'split' very quickly and you must apply it as quickly as possible. A crackle glaze effect allows the base colour to be seen through the top colour on the exterior of the unit so the base colour was a particularly important consideration. When the effect was quite dry, I antiqued the outside of the cupboard further by rubbing coloured antiquing wax all over the surface so that some wax was held in the cracks and some colour penetrated the absorbent emulsion colour. As well as giving this wonderful patina of age to the whole unit, the wax also serves as a protective layer.

The stamping designs I used for the inside of the cupboard were very simple flower and leaf motifs that I chose for their very simplicity. I used one stamp design as a garland at the top of the cupboard and a simpler floral motif was used as a repeat pattern for the inside of the cupboard in contrasting colours.

1 Using an old paintbrush, apply a liberal amount of paint stripper all over the exterior of the cupboard. Use a dabbing motion to apply the stripper onto the surface, rather than brushing it, as this helps to make the stripping process much easier. Protect your hands and work outside, if at all possible.

2 When the stripper has had time to work (always refer to the manufacturer's instructions), it will start to blister away at the old surface. Once this has occurred, start to strip away at the old paint, varnish and stripper with a stripping knife to reveal the bare wood that is underneath.

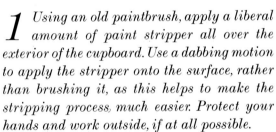

3 Once the surface is completely clear, wipe the cupboard over with a damp cloth soaked with a little vinegar to remove any remaining stripper. Leave to dry for a few hours or until surface-dry, then paint the whole surface inside and out with a layer of acrylic primer.

4 When the primer is dry (30 minutes to an hour), apply the first emulsion layer to the exterior with a household brush. In this case, I used a yellow ochre colour. When totally dry (30 minutes to one hour), apply transparent crackle glaze over the dry base coat with a suitably-sized paintbrush.

5 *After approximately an hour, the glaze will be completely dry. Working a section at a time, apply the top coat over the glaze using a wide 7.5 cm (3 in) paintbrush. Try to work as quickly as possible, as the peeling effect starts to happen soon after contact with the paint.*

6 *Apply off-white emulsion to cover the interior of the cupboard. When the crackle effect is completely dry (about two to three hours or leave overnight), use a soft cloth to gently rub antiquing wax into the surface of the wood. The wax will have a darkening effect on the paint.*

RIGHT. *To paint the fine glazing panels for the cupboard, I taped around the edges of the glass using masking tape for quick and easy painting of the top coat emulsion. Once the glazing bars were dry, I removed the tape. Any stray paint marks were carefully scraped from the glass using the sharp edge of a Stanley knife blade, but do protect your fingers from the sharp edge if you need to use one.*

The inside of the cupboard and the shelves were sealed with a protective coat of acrylic varnish to guard against knocks and scrapes. Once this was dry (about an hour), the cupboard was hung on the wall using strong screw fixings. Due to the heavy nature of a cupboard such as this one, we needed to use heavy-duty fixings to make sure it was completely secure and wouldn't fall down once all the china and glass was inside. For the final touch, a replacement handle was fixed onto one of the doors.

7 *Use a tape measure to determine the exact positioning of the first stamp and mark this position with chalk or pencil. Load the stamp in the usual way (see page 35). Print the motif onto the back of the unit following the chalked or pencilled guide lines. (Here I used a deep pink colour.)*

8 *Finally, load the second stamp with a contrasting colour (here I used a dark blue shade) and then stamp this motif between the garlands created by the first stamp. Continue using this second stamp over the back of the unit to create a regular, repeating pattern across the cupboard.*

LEFT. *The wooden candlesticks were first given a simple, distressed paint finish using the candle wax resist method (see page 25). I used an off-white top colour, similar to the wall cupboard (see page 49), over a sage green base colour. A tiny leaf stamp (see page 50) was printed around the candlestick base to complement the* leaves that were stamped inside the cupboard. Once the motifs were dry, I then applied a little antiquing wax over the surface of the candlestick to deepen the colours and also to protect the painted surface from any knocks.

The placemats were made by sewing a stamped linen panel (see page 122) over a slightly larger, woven fabric rectangle. Always use specialist fabric colours (see page 18) as these will 'bond' to the fabric, whereas other colours will wash away when cleaned. As you stitch the linen over the base fabric, turn the raw edges under to prevent them from fraying. Press the cloth to seal the colour, then tease the threads from the edges of the woven fabric to fray the sides.

ABOVE. *I used two stamps to decorate this plain china (see page 118). Always use ceramic colours (see page 19) if you intend to use the china and, although these are washable, the china shouldn't be used on an everyday basis and it will not stand up to the rigours of a dishwasher.* Ceramic colours are available from good art suppliers and there are two types available. One paint requires the hot temperature of an oven in order to bake the paint. Once the colour is stamped onto the ceramics, they are then placed in an oven at a high temperature for approximately half an hour. The second type of ceramic colour is perhaps less durable, as this is simply left to dry normally without the need for heat. I would suggest that this type of colour should only be used for decorative china pieces and certainly not for those pieces that are intended to be used.

LEFT. *The tray was made from plain, undecorated* MDF *(medium-density fibreboard), which simply required a quick coat of acrylic primer before painting. Once again, to complement the rustic style of the kitchen, the colours were distressed, then antiqued with wax (see page 27). The creamy-coloured base coat was applied over the base and sides of the tray, both inside and out. Once dry, candle wax was rubbed vigorously over the sides. Next, a sage green top coat was painted over the wax and, when dry, the colours were distressed to give this beautiful effect.*

When the painting was completed, two different stamps (see page 118) were used to create this pattern using terracotta red and sage green colours and, because this tray is wider than most, I stamped two columns of the design. For a narrower tray, you may wish to stamp one central column.

Once the stamped colours were dry I lightly rubbed coloured wax over the surface of the tray to deepen the colours and also to lend an antique finish to the overall effect.

ABOVE. *This bottle rack was also made from unfinished* MDF, *which is simple to prepare. A coat of white acrylic primer is all that is needed. Rich colours were used for the distressed paint effect – a deep Shaker blue and a terracotta red. The red was applied first, covering the white primer. Next, a layer of candle wax was rubbed over the surface of the dry paint and then the blue top coat was applied. Abrasive paper was used to distress the two colours to reach a satisfactory result (see page 25).*

I used two small stamps to build up the pattern on the rack – a small flower from the wall cupboard (see page 49), and the small leaf which was used around the candlestick bases (see page 50). A layer of coloured wax was then rubbed over the bottle rack using a soft cloth to deepen the colours and protect the surface.

PRINTED CUPBOARD

MATERIALS: *An old or new cupboard, screwdriver, medium- and fine-grade abrasive papers, electric sander, filler, 2.5 cm (1 in) and 5 cm (2 in) paintbrushes plus an artist's brush, paint kettle, acrylic primer/sealer, sage green and grey emulsions, scumble glaze, ruler, pencil, right-angle measure, plate, square motif stamp (see page 123), acrylic varnish and new handles.*

This old kitchen cupboard is one of a set of three cupboards. The chipped, red formica tops were in a very bad state, so I wanted to replace them. I decided on a tough and hard-wearing tiled mosaic surface effect, but there are many alternatives that you can consider. If you can unscrew the entire worktop away from the cupboard, then you can replace it with almost anything. A selection of natural slate or marble is a possibility, although this could be expensive. A solid wood worktop, or simply a cut piece of plywood in almost any colour, is another alternative solution. Larger tiles may be difficult to cut, so if you really like the idea of a tiled work surface, hunt for tiny mosaic

tiles, which are far easier to lay. I also replaced the handles, which dramatically altered the final piece.

Before you can even begin to think about transforming the cupboard surface, you must prepare it for painting first. If the surface is waxed, remove as much as you can by rubbing with wire wool and turpentine. To prepare a painted surface, remove all flaking paint and 'key' it with coarse, medium and then fine abrasive paper. Use a soft, dappled scumble glaze over the base coat to cover the surface of the furniture and to create an interesting background for stamping.

I love to stamp over a broken colour, rather than simply stamping over a flat, uninteresting one. It really does seem to add definition to the piece of furniture and to make it seem rather more important than its humble origins. To create this type of glaze, you will need to purchase a commercially prepared scumble glaze. This is available from good decorating stores, as well as some art and craft suppliers. It is worth remembering that a little glaze goes a long way. Mix together an equal amount of glaze to paint colour and stir well. Then scrub the glaze sparingly with a paintbrush over the entire painted surface to colour it, creating a dappled effect. Allow this to dry completely before stamping over the top.

When stamping in a regular pattern, it is important to establish a grid for each stamp. Arbitrary placing of stamps will result in haphazard-looking furniture. Once I had decided that the stamped area would be centrally placed inside the cupboard doors, I marked this up with a right-angle measure, ruler and pencil, taking my pattern into account. I didn't worry about making pencil marks over the painted surface as I knew that these would be disguised later on with a finely painted line.

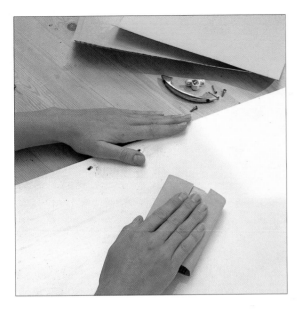

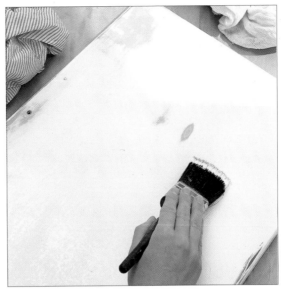

1 Remove any handles and take the doors off the cupboard, if possible. Give painted or varnished furniture a good sanding down with medium-grade, then fine-grade abrasive papers to provide a 'key' for the base coat of paint. For larger pieces of furniture, use an electric sander.

2 Surface holes in the wood should be filled, then brush on one coat of acrylic primer/sealer. This will provide a base for the subsequent layers of colour. Leave to dry thoroughly, according to the manufacturer's instructions, leaving drawers open and doors ajar if they are impossible to remove first.

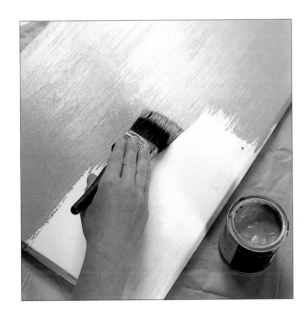

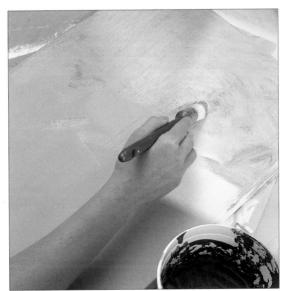

3 Apply the sage green base coat evenly all over the primed surface and let dry (about 30 minutes to an hour). If the coat dries unevenly or brush marks are still visible, then apply a second coat of paint. However, make sure the first coat of paint is thoroughly dry before you begin to do this.

4 In a paint kettle, mix together a little of the grey colour (this is later used for stamping) with an equal amount of scumble glaze for the top coat. (Acrylic varnish can be used in place of scumble glaze if necessary.) Then work this unevenly over the whole surface of the cupboard.

5 *When the glaze has completely dried, start to mark out the margins of the area that are to be stamped with a ruler, pencil and right-angle measure. Measure the stamp, then mark on the appropriate dimensions, to determine the number of prints that are needed to cover your piece of furniture.*

6 *Paint a little of the stamping colour onto a flat surface (an old plate is ideal) to provide an even layer of colour to press your stamp into. Hold the stamp at the sides, then press firmly into the paint and lift out. Press again, if unevenly coated. Test on a scrap of paper first.*

RIGHT. *This kitchen cupboard was given a sage green emulsion base coat, followed by a dappled coat of scumble glaze tinted with the grey colour that was used for stamping prior to applying the stamps. Once the stamped designs were printed onto the cupboard, a fine grey line (see page 31) was painted around the stamped area to distinguish the design, making the cupboard even more striking. Once dry, a coat of acrylic varnish was applied over the painted surface to protect it from damage and also to make cleaning much easier (an important consideration here).*

Old junk-shop finds are affordable pieces of furniture that are not too precious to discourage anyone from 'having a go' at stamping, and the results can be just as stunning as the project featured opposite.

7 *Position the stamp on the surface of the cupboard, using the outline marked on the back to align the motif correctly. Once the stamp is in the right position, apply firm (but direct) pressure to the back of the stamp with your palm and then hold this in place for a few seconds.*

8 *When the stamping has been completed, allow the surface to dry thoroughly (about an hour). For a professional finish, use an artist's brush to paint a thin line around the margins of the stamped area. Protect and seal with acrylic varnish, when the line is dry.*

LEFT. *This heavy pine table was made of bare, untreated wood, which meant that I was able to start immediately with my decorative paint treatment, rather than laboriously stripping away any previous coverings. Often this type of farmhouse-style furniture is simply treated with a coloured wax. To remove this, you should rub the surface with a pad of wire wool soaked in white spirit until all traces of the wax are removed.*

The stamps used for the serving tray (see pages 52–53) were put to use along the sides of this table. I had decided to use the same colours as before: a dull terracotta for the leaves and a greyish green for the stylized stalk. And because the sides of a table are rather narrow, I stamped the leaves first, fitting these into the space, then adding the stalks in afterwards, squeezing them between the remaining spaces. Turned details on the legs were distressed in sage green emulsion and, to finish, the base of the table was rubbed with antique wax for protection.

LEFT. *This tall bread box was simply decorated using the same two small stamps that were used for the creamy coloured ceramics (see pages 51 and 118), although here I used emulsion colours on the wooden surface, whereas the ceramics were stamped with ceramic paints (see page 19).*

The background colour was quick to prepare using a colour washed effect (see page 22) with colours that are very close in tone (pale and sunny yellows) to produce a soft, cloudy effect. This provided a perfect background for the silvery greys and greens of the olive sprigs. The leaves of the olive sprigs were first stamped around the box top using a variety of similar leaf colours. Olive green is mixed with black and white to vary the tone of the leaves. Squeeze a little of the basic colour onto a mixing palette and, next to this, squeeze some white and black. For each stamp, mix a little black or white into the base colour to alter it slightly from the previous one to give a hand-finished effect. Stamp the olives last of all using purplish and olive green colours, then finish off with a layer of acrylic varnish to seal.

The LIVING ROOM

Rich plum, ochre and spice colours have all been combined here to create a living room with an ethnic feel. The stamp designs are strong and daring, and make a powerful decorative backdrop for a room that features furniture and accessories in striking wrought iron and heavily-carved woodwork.

The bold stamp used on these walls is a far cry from the floral designs that we are likely to see in many of our living rooms. Here the stamped pattern is contained within painted panels and the overall effect has the appearance of an expensive hand-blocked wallpaper. It has a wonderfully textured finish that is particularly appealing and, rather than striving for a perfect print every time, the stamp can be uneven, occasionally missing out part of the design. This accentuates the hand-crafted quality that works brilliantly in this particular room.

PLANTATION-STYLE WALL FINISH

MATERIALS: *Household paintbrush, base and top coat emulsion paints in mid-toned ochre colours, paint kettle, decorator's sponge, tape measure, chalk, plumb line, masking tape, midnight blue emulsion paint, 2.5 cm (1 in) paintbrush, dark ochre emulsion paint, stamps (see pages 121 and 123), glass sheet, emulsion paintbrush (7.5 cm/3 in), darker line colour and line painting brush (2.5 cm/1 in).*

Stamping is perfect for wall finishes as it gives the appearance of a rather expensive, hand-blocked wallpaper. The inspiration for this design came from looking at exactly this kind of wallpaper, which was used for a grand house and featured in one of the magazines on interiors. The whole look has a kind of *Out of Africa* quality about it that is particularly appealing. Although it may look rather complicated, this motif is easy to cut into shape from the foam rubber and, once glued to the block, it is used in the same way as any other stamp. However, you may find the actual printing

process (when the block is pressed onto the surface of the wall) is much easier if two people press together on the back of the block. This helps in two ways: first, it is less work to push on the block if there are two pairs of hands working together and secondly, it helps to prevent the block from slipping, which it is sometimes prone to do on a vertical surface.

The stamp is printed inside painted panels, which are simple to plot out on the walls using a retractable tape measure. Plan the positions of the panels first by dividing the number of panels into the length of the wall, making allowances for the gaps between each panel. Plot the resulting measurements onto the wall using white chalk, then use masking tape to seal off the area to make the fine lines.

When loading a large stamp, you will find it easier to brush the paint over a glass sheet rather than a plate, as the size is much better accommodated and also offers a more even coverage. A large plate inevitably curves upwards around the rim, preventing the whole block from touching the paint. For loading the block, a regular piece of window glass is perfectly adequate, provided that you cover the sharp edges neatly with masking tape to prevent any accidents.

Here a paint effect has been created for this stamp, but you may already have painted walls on which to print the stamp directly. Walls that have a solid colour rather than a paint effect could also work well although I tend to favour walls with the character of a paint finish. Simple wall washes are easy and, as the room is already prepared with dust sheets, why not spend a few more hours applying a quick wall wash to prepare a perfect background?

1 Paint the wall with a solid coat of your chosen base colour with a household brush. In this particular case, a mid-yellow ochre colour was used. If necessary, apply a second coat of paint to achieve a good, even coverage. Allow to dry for at least an hour between the two coats.

2 Decant a little of the second colour into a paint kettle. Here I used a darker tone of the base colour and then thinned it out with an equal quantity of water. Scrub the walls with the diluted colour using a cellulose decorator's sponge to gradually build up a rather cloudy-looking effect.

3 Mark up the walls to create the panels around the room, using a retractable tape measure and white chalk. Keep checking the verticals with a plumb line as you go round the room as your walls may not be perfectly straight. Then carefully mask along the edge of the chalk lines.

4 Paint between the masked areas using a strong colour and with a 2.5 cm (1 in) paintbrush. (I used midnight blue.) A finer line is painted outside this panel using a different colour (here darkest ochre emulsion, which I later used for stamping), but with the same technique.

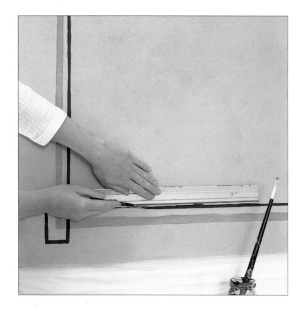

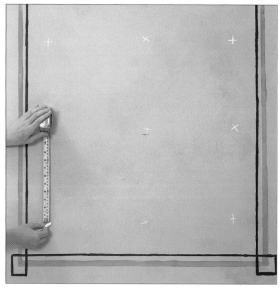

5 You may wish to add a painted square at the corner of each of the blue-painted panels to give further definition. Extend these painted lines outwards to go beyond the panel and then finish them off in a neat square. Use masking tape to help you to achieve much cleaner lines.

6 Use a retractable tape measure to perfect-ly plot out the positions of the stamps. Measure both the height and width of each of the panels to determine exactly the right num-ber of stamps that are needed and then plot the centre of each stamp onto the wall using chalk, which can be easily removed later on.

RIGHT. *In this room I decided to print the stamped motifs inside the painted panels, rather than as an all-over pattern. A colour washed ochre paint finish (see page 22) provides the dappled background onto which the deeper ochre stamps are positioned. The larger, quite intricate motifs are interspersed with a much smaller secondary stamp, which balances the overall pattern. If too many motifs were stamped with the larger block, this would make the pattern appear overcrowded, whereas too few would seem too sparse.*

The simple, painted lines provide neat, unfussy panels which frame the stamps perfectly. A suitably exotic potted palm adds to the plantation style and evokes a certain tropical air, while a cushion in complementary prints (see page 73) and silk scarf on the sofa, as well as an intriguing pot, all add interesting details to the overall look of the room.

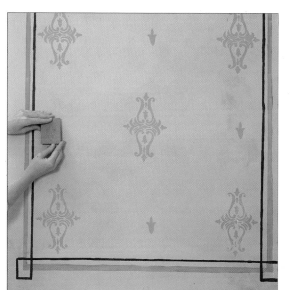

7 Load the stamp (I used darkest ochre emulsion here) in the usual way (see page 35) and press it onto the wall. It may even be necessary for two people to press onto the back of the stamp to transfer the paint evenly onto the wall, as this stamp is much larger than most.

8 Once the larger stamps are printed, fill in any remaining gaps with the second, smaller stamp design, again with darkest ochre paint. Some parts of the two stamps may not print perfectly, but this should not detract from the overall effect of an elegantly hand-blocked paper.

LEFT. *A full-length tablecloth and a smaller protective cloth are simply made from washable cotton fabrics. The larger cloth required two lengths of fabric, which were joined together along the long edges and the seam lay across the centre of the table. Dressmakers' pins were used to mark the point where the fabric just touched the floor.*

The fabric was lifted off the table and the hemline was cut, using the pins as a guide. It was then sewn, turning the raw edges underneath in a double hem to prevent fraying. Next, the smaller, top cloth was made from just a single length of fabric, which was cut into a square. The ends were sewn as before, using a double hem to prevent the fabric from fraying.

Decorative stamps helped to enforce the Out of Africa *feeling using a bold abstract pattern and a stylized leaf in fabric colours. (For these templates, refer to pages 119 and 120.)*

LEFT. *This shaped planter was simply constructed from* MDF *(medium-density fibreboard). The plain, flat sides were perfect for one of the larger stamps used for the wall treatment (see page 65) and I finished off the edges with a fine hand-painted line, which neatly completed the overall look. Here the colours used were exactly the same as those I had selected for the walls, although for the base colour I decided to paint only one colour to give a flat finish, rather than the colour washed effect seen on the walls.*

The planter, although originally intended to disguise ugly plant containers, is used for dried plants. But it also makes a great storage container for magazines and newspapers, as well as being a stylish waste bin. Seal the planter both inside and out with varnish for a wipe-clean, protected surface.

CRACKLE-VARNISHED LIGHT BASE

MATERIALS:

Lampshade, acrylic white primer/sealer, paint kettle, (2.5 cm/1 in) paintbrushes, masking tape, mid-tone terracotta red emulsion, off-white top coat emulsion, two soft cloths, decorator's or sea sponge, tea bags, leaf pattern stamp (see page 118), plate, chalk or soft pencil, two-part crackle varnish, burnt umber oil colour and gilding cream.

The basic MDF (medium-density fibreboard) construction of this lamp base is perfect for a textured paint effect. When viewed from close up, the paint effect has a wonderfully crazed, antique finish. This was, in fact, created quite simply but rather unusually, by first brushing a creamy off-white colour over a reddish base colour. Then, before the paint began to dry, the whole surface was splashed with water and an absorbent cloth was quickly pressed over the wet, splattered surface. When the cloth was lifted off, it took away with it some of the

top colour to reveal spots of the base colour underneath. The paint effect works well on small items, but it would be much harder to manage on larger projects. To control the effect, work a small section at a time to avoid the top colour drying out too rapidly.

After the stamp is printed on the flat parts of the lamp base, the whole thing is then crackle-varnished *(see page 30)*. The two-part varnish creates a fine network of cracks over the surface of the lamp and, although these are not clearly visible to the eye, when raw umber artist's oil colour is rubbed into the surface the crazed surface is clearly highlighted. As a finishing touch, a little gilding cream was rubbed into the raised section around the base of the lamp using a soft cloth.

A new and pristine shade would have looked too clumsy on the antiqued base and so a wash of strong cold tea was applied over the whole shade for an instant aged effect. Simply wipe the tea over the shade using the sponge as if you were wiping it clean. Recharge the sponge with tea, when required. Tea lends a soft parchment quality to fabric or paper shades to knock the edge off their unfashionable newness.

When positioning the stamps around the edge of the shade, it helps to view the shade from above and to mark the positions of a clock face along the outer edge with chalk. Use each of these marks as your centre line for placing the leaf stamps. Roll the stamps around the shade to transfer the paint evenly. Hold one hand inside the shade and use a little pressure here against the stamp to get a good print. Roll the block over the shade and lift off. Take care not to smudge the stamped motifs as you print the remaining patterns. The emulsion paint should be dry within half an hour.

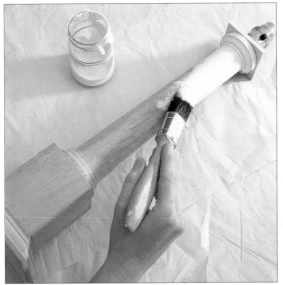

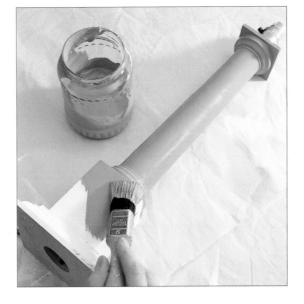

1 Prime the lamp base with white acrylic primer (one coat should be sufficient to give an even coverage), using a small brush. Use masking tape to protect the brass light holder and the electric cable to avoid these being painted. Leave to dry for 30 minutes to an hour.

2 Clean the brush and then carefully apply an even coat of the base colour. (I used a mid-tone, terracotta red emulsion, which was chosen as a strong contrast between the off-white top coat.) Again, one coat of paint should be sufficient. Leave this to dry for 30 minutes to an hour.

3 Apply a top coat with a clean brush, one section at a time. While wet, flick water over the surface using your fingertips. Allow this to rest on the surface for about a minute, then dab with a dry cloth. Using a decorator's or a sea sponge, smooth the top coat over the lamp base.

4 Next, gently brush a strong tea solution over the whole of the fabric shade to give an antiqued look. Leave the shade in a warm place to dry thoroughly (about 30 minutes). While the shade is drying, stamp the lamp base with the leaf pattern in the terracotta base colour.

5 Mark the positions of the stamp around the base of the shade using either chalk or a feint pencil mark. Load the stamp (see page 18) and position it directly onto the shade. Place your other hand inside the shade to make a firm contact with the stamp so that pressure is evenly applied.

6 Once the lamp base is dry, apply the first stage of the crackle varnish (see page 30). Allow this to dry according to the manufacturer's recommendations, as these varnishes all vary slightly. Use a 2.5 cm (1 in) decorator's brush, then apply the second varnish with the same (cleaned) brush.

RIGHT. *Here the fabric shade has been given a parchment quality by applying a simple wash of cold tea evenly and quickly over the whole surface. Once dry (after 30 minutes), the delicate leaf motifs (see page 118) are stamped around the shade. The same stamp has also been used at the lamp base and this colour has been knocked back on the base to unify the whole look of the lamp.*

Crackle varnish is easy to use (see page 30) and adds an instant patina of age over everything onto which it is applied. This lamp is no exception: the delicately crazed surface gives a new paint finish a sense of old age and antiquity that is so very appealing to the eye.

7 When the second coat of crackle varnish has dried (allow two to three hours), you may see a myriad of tiny cracks appear over the surface of the varnish. To make these cracks more visible, rub burnt umber oil colour all over the surface of the varnish using a soft cloth.

8 Finally, to complete the aged look, rub a small amount of gold gilt cream over all of the raised parts of the lamp base to highlight the fine surface cracks. Use your fingers to apply the wax then, when this is dry, buff it up with a clean cloth and then replace the shade over the base.

BELOW. *The trinket box uses the same stamp as featured on the walls (see pages 62–65), but in a slightly unusual way. Stamp exactly one-half of the motif at each corner of the box, then turn it around and stamp the other half on the other side* of the corner. *Continue in this way until all four corners of the box are printed and then stamp one whole motif on top of the box lid. The yellow ochre motifs are stamped over a deep plum base coat and finished with the crackle varnish effect (see* page 30). *Highlight the tiny cracks with dark antiquing wax rubbed in with a soft cloth.*

The storage tray has been treated in a similar way to the trinket box, but this time the colours have been reversed out to give a slightly different look.

RIGHT. *The pieces for each of these cushions should be cut out, then stamped first using fabric colours (see pages 18 and 123). First iron the fabric and spread it out over newspaper sheets. Mark out the positions of the stamp* with chalk, then print in the usual way. Once the fabric paint is dry, it can be fixed using a hot iron gently pressed over the reverse of the fabric.

Cut three pieces of fabric for each cushion – the front should be 2.5 cm (1 in) larger all round than the pad. The back of the cushion is made from two pieces of fabric, both three-quarters of the size of the front to make an envelope closing. Sew piped cord between the seam for a tailored finish.

The
BEDROOM

The colours of this room are largely influenced by the Swedish style of decorating. Natural light filters into the room and informal details reinforce the feeling of a calm and relaxing environment. Nothing seems laboured in this room; there are no fussy swags, drapes or frilly details, and the whole feeling is refreshing and peaceful. This is a place to wind down and sleep in, or a soothing place in which to wake up and feel energized.

Bedrooms are private, intimate areas, and creating your own space away from a ringing telephone or noisy children can be immensely indulgent and uplifting. The gentle pinky tones on the walls are softly colour washed with paints that are close in tone, while the stamped colours are equally soft and harmonious using a silvery green colour. Furniture is also treated with a delicate, complementary palette to reflect the surrounding colours. Nothing jars in this room or interrupts the feeling of calm. Many of the surfaces are stamped, but the overall effect never becomes overpowering.

Choose plants and cut flowers that are heavily scented, such as long-stemmed lilies, jasmine and lilac. Delicate flowers with lots of greenery are preferable to the hothouse variety. Be prepared to indulge yourself.

SCANDINAVIAN DRESSING TABLE

MATERIALS: *Dressing table and panels, mirror, cloth, paint kettle, white primer, 5 cm (2 in) rounded paintbrush, buff base, dark blue and dark grey top coat, old brush for mixing, chalk, off-white emulsion, plate, floral and chain stamps* (see pages 119 and 125), *artist's brush, masking tape, gouache, acrylic varnish and two piano-type hinges.*

Blank MDF (medium-density fibreboard) furniture is perfect for this type of decoration. The smooth surface is wonderful for almost every paint finish and paint goes on easily and effortlessly, resulting in a perfect finish every time. There are a number of suppliers around who specialize in producing this type of blank furniture. Their details can be found in the classified advertising sections of various home interest magazines and we have listed some of these in the Suppliers section of this book *(see page 126).* You may also find undecorated furniture in some DIY stores and larger home furnishing stores.

For this particular dressing table project, I used an unusual table with pretty Queen Anne style legs. It could be used equally well in other rooms of the house as an occasional table. However, when topped with a three-panelled screen, it makes an attractive piece of bedroom furniture.

There is a feeling of sophistication and elegance in this bedroom. The colours are largely influenced by the Scandinavian style of decoration. Cool shades and lots of reflected light make this room a place to unwind and rest. The stamped leaves featured over the walls are delicate and unobtrusive, although they are quite large in scale. They were applied randomly to give a relaxed appearance.

The pattern chosen for the side of the dressing table was inspired by a piece of Swedish furniture. It comprises a floral motif linked together with an interlocking chain pattern. The table was first given a basic paint finish and the stamped design was then applied over this. When planning the size of the stamps, the sides of the table should be taken into account. Divide the length of the longest section by the number of interlocking chain motifs required. You can then adjust the scale of the stamp design to suit. When choosing a piece of furniture for use as a dressing table, look for one that has deep sides, which are large enough to feature a strong decorative treatment like this.

Dressing-table tops invariably become cluttered and any decoration will soon become unseen, so I finished this one off with simple line and corner flourishes.

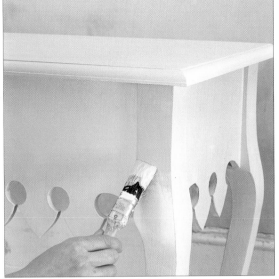

1 Wipe the surface of the table down using a damp cloth to remove any dust. Then paint over the whole surface using white acrylic primer. Brush the paint out thinly and evenly with long strokes, making sure that you reach into all the nooks and crannies using a 5 cm (2 in) decorator's brush.

2 When the primer is completely dry (about 30 minutes to an hour), apply the coloured base coat emulsion. (A buff colour was chosen for this project.) You may need to apply two coats (allow 30 minutes to an hour between coats) for even coverage with none of the white primer showing through.

3 Mix together the two parts of the top coat (dark blue and grey used here) with one part water, and apply this roughly over the dried base coat. Use a rounded brush for this and work in a scrubbing motion. Aim to build up a dappled paint effect with some base colour showing through.

4 Use chalk to measure and mark out the positions of the larger linking motif onto the side of the table. Take these as guide lines for stamping. Pour off-white emulsion onto a plate and load the stamp with a small amount of paint. Press down and repeat the next pattern alongside the first.

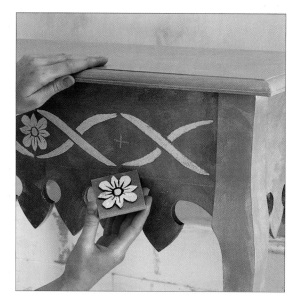

5 *Use chalk to mark the centre of each link in the chained pattern and position the centre of the flower stamp directly over this. Press the stamp onto the side of the table with an even, but firm pressure. Lift it off and then repeat the pattern all the way along the border of the table.*

6 *Paint a fine narrow line around the top of the dressing table to create a neatly finished edge. If you don't have a steady hand, use masking tape to achieve a straight line. Make sure you secure the tape lightly so that it doesn't take the paint off when you go to remove it later on.*

RIGHT. *The mirror is made up from a basic three-panelled screen joined together with piano hinges. I chose the same background colour for the screen as the base colour on the table. Rather than using the same stamp as for the table, I chose an alternative stamp (see page 118) used elsewhere in the room so as not to appear too contrived or co-ordinated. The shaped mirror was cut by a glass merchant. Always remember to have the edges ground by your supplier, otherwise they could remain dangerously sharp. The mirror was fixed into place using a strong epoxy resin adhesive.*

A similar (but smaller) leaf was also stamped onto the surface of the small jewellery box. Due to the inevitable wear and tear on a box like this, the painted surface has also been treated with an application of coloured furniture wax. This enriches the colour of the paint layers, as well as protecting the surface.

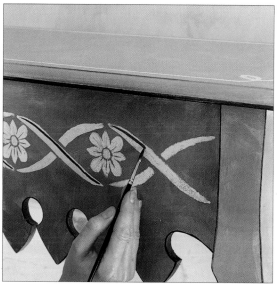

7 *Rather than joining the lines in each corner, a small flourish finishes off the effect and is easy to achieve. Use chalk to draw two small semi-circles curving in from the painted lines, then paint over with a fine brush. You can rest your hand on the table top to steady it, if you need some support.*

8 *Use a fine artist's brush and a little gouache colour (dark blue used here), thinned with water, to add detailing to the stamped effect. Accentuate the shaped edge of the table with the same colour. Once dry, add at least one coat of acrylic varnish to protect the surface and to seal the colours.*

LEFT. *The soft, reflective colours of this bedroom are illustrated in a still life on a side table. Here the surfaces are all stamped, but they are in no way intrusive or over-the-top. Subtle colours and simple shapes all help to create the elegance and charm that is so characteristic in this wonderfully calming style of room.*

A casual bed throw, made from natural woven linen, is patterned with the same linking stamped design used for the dressing table (see Stamp Designs, pages 119 and 125). This time, however, the stamped colours are changed to a deep blood-red and printed using fabric colour (see page 18). A scalloped border elevates the casual throw into something more elegant and eye-catching. Each scallop's curve is marked out with the rim of a teacup and these are then sewn, trimmed and turned to the right side before they are stitched onto the edge of the printed linen throw.

A hand-painted flourish, representing the stem from each leaf, provides an elegant effect over the soft, dappled bedroom walls.

LEFT. *Flat-fronted picture frames are perfect for a stamped decorative treatment as there are no fussy details or mouldings to get in the way. This understated, spiralling leafy motif (see page 123) adds a certain vitality to the frame without being too fussy. Here ordinary white emulsion colour will work perfectly well for stamping, provided that the underlying surface is 'keyed' lightly with fine abrasive paper. A layer of acrylic varnish over the dried design will ensure the stamp stays put, particularly when the dusting cloth appears!*

Frame your favourite snap shots or drawings, or build up your own composite picture from cut-out black and white images pasted over scribbled background paper. Flat-fronted frames are readily available from many stores; some are plain, natural wood frames, while others may be painted or stained. When using coloured frames, make sure that the stamping colour you decide to use is in a strong contrast to the colour of the frame.

MUSLIN BLINDS

MATERIALS: *Iron, dressmaker's scissors, tape measure, muslin for front and back of blinds (roughly cut to size), absorbent paper, masking tape, pencil, straight-edged ruler, stamp (see motifs, page 122), fabric paint (I mixed white with a little yellow and blue), plate, dressmaker's pins, needle and white thread, sewing machine, touch-and-close fastener, dowelling rods, handsaw, abrasive paper, curtain rings, cord and cleats (for fixing).*

These Roman blinds are constructed from inexpensive, ordinary cotton muslin. The double thickness of fabric allows a certain amount of privacy whilst still letting the natural light filter into the room. To hold the folds perfectly in shape, neat, parallel rows of dowelling are required and these are clearly visible from the front of the blind, particularly when the sun shines, but they are far from a distraction. The dowelling rows add a certain interest to the flimsy fabric. As the light filters through, the stamped motifs appear to be little silhouettes against the light and the whole effect is very charming.

The construction of blinds is quite straightforward. First, take an accurate measurement of the finished width and drop of the blind. It could hang either inside or outside a window recess – it's really up to you and this will depend on your particular window and its shape. Once this measurement is determined, cut the pieces of muslin accordingly. You will need to work on a large, flat surface and the fabric should be pressed and laid out flat. Because of the flimsy nature of muslin, you should take extra care to keep the fabric as flat as possible to cut out accurately otherwise you'll end up with wobbly seams.

Cut the fabric using your own window measurements, but add 2.5 cm (1 in) all around for a good seam allowance. You will need to cut two pieces of muslin for each blind and these should be exactly the same size. Reserve one thickness of muslin and place the other over a newspaper-covered table top. Mark out the positions of the stamp motif clearly on the surface of the muslin using a soft pencil and a ruler. The stamp is loaded in the usual way using fabric paints. I mixed a little yellow and blue fabric colour into the white base to achieve a slightly off-white fabric colour. Use the chalk registration marks as a guide for printing and continue stamping until the whole piece of fabric is printed.

Once the paint has dried, the blinds are made up according to the step-by-step instructions. To hang the blinds up at the windows, you will need to screw a wooden batten across the top of the window frame. On the front edge of the batten, staple or tack one-half of a touch-and-close fastener. Fix screw-in brass eyes along the bottom edge of the batten to align with the rings sewn onto the blind. The other fastener half is sewn onto the top of the blind. When pressed together, these two parts hold the blind in place.

1 Press the muslin fabric using a warm iron to remove all the creases. Cut the fabric approximately to size leaving a generous allowance all round (at least 10 cm/4 in). Lay the fabric over a table top protected with absorbent paper and tape this securely in place with masking tape.

2 Next, mark out the positions for each of the stamp motifs clearly onto the muslin using a soft pencil. Use a straight-edged ruler for the most precise measuring. When you are doing this, be careful that the first motif won't be cut in half later on once the fabric is cut out more accurately.

3 Load the stamp in the usual way (see page 18) and start printing. The masking tape will prevent the muslin from moving around whilst stamping is taking place, and the absorbent paper placed under the fabric will prevent any damage being caused to the table top underneath.

4 Allow the fabric to dry according to the paint manufacturer's instructions, then remove the masking tape and press with a warm iron. Lay the fabric over the table and cut to size. Use the measurements for your window, plus 2.5 cm (1 in) all round for a seam allowance.

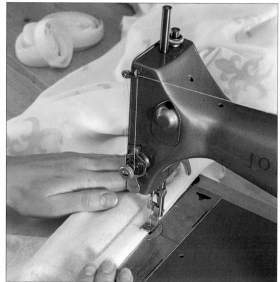

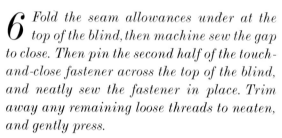

5 Pin, tack and then machine stitch the front and back pieces of the blind together, keeping right sides facing and the raw edges together. Leave the top edge open for turning through to the right side. Carefully trim the seam allowance, turn and then press with a warm iron.

6 Fold the seam allowances under at the top of the blind, then machine sew the gap to close. Then pin the second half of the touch-and-close fastener across the top of the blind, and neatly sew the fastener in place. Trim away any remaining loose threads to neaten, and gently press.

7 Cut up strips of muslin to measure 10 cm (4 in) deep and the width of the blind, plus an allowance of 2.5 cm (1 in) for the end hems. These will make up the dowelling casings. Fold the strips in half lengthwise and sew across a long and short side. Then turn the fabric through to the right side.

8 Lay the blind flat on your table top and mark a horizontal line to measure about 10 cm (4 in) from the bottom and 25 cm (10 in) from the top of the blind. Divide the remaining measurement by the required number of rods. Then draw in the horizontal lines accordingly using a soft pencil.

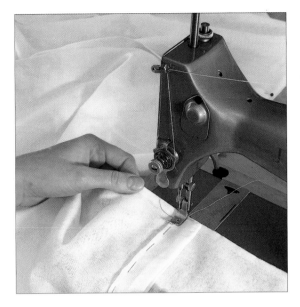

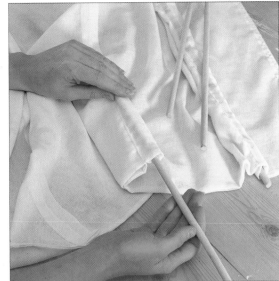

9 Pin one edge of the rod pocket over the horizontal line. Repeat this procedure for the other rod pockets, keeping the blind as flat as possible and the seams horizontal. Then machine stitch the pocket to the blind with the stitching line positioned close to the edge of the fabric.

10 Cut the dowelling rods to size with a small handsaw: these should measure the width of the blind less 2.5 cm (1 in). Sand the ends with abrasive paper to remove any splinters. Insert the rod into the pocket and hand stitch the small gap closed with just a few stitches to secure.

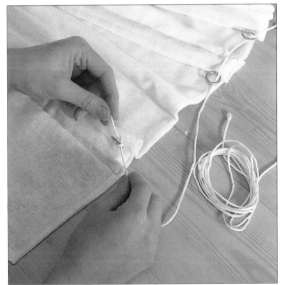

11 Carefully sew the curtain rings to the bottom edge of each fabric casing by hand leaving intervals of 51 cm (20 in) and 2.5 cm (1 in) in from each edge. To achieve the most accurate placement, mark out these points first, using a straight-edged ruler and soft pencil.

12 Thread cord through the rings, taking the cords to one side and tie these together, then thread through the eyes onto the batten, and tie around a cleat fixed to the wall to hold. Pull into neat, crisp folds with the cords. (If you wish, a wooden acorn could be threaded onto the ends of the cords to neaten.)

LEFT. *Blinds like these, made from diaphanous muslin that allows the light to filter through, can be left permanently closed, if necessary. They offer a solution to privacy without the need to obscure light. The blinds are both practical and smart, and the stamped design is printed with fabric colours which means they are fully machine washable (see page 18). Unpick the hand-sewn ends to remove the dowelling rods prior to washing. The fabric will inevitably crease up during the washing process but it can be quickly ironed back into shape afterwards.*

Keep the shapes simple: use the same stamp I used here or choose your own, and print with off-white colours. Remember that fabric colours can be successfully mixed together; blend white with dark colours to produce softer and creamier shades of off-white.

LEFT. *A creamy-coloured fabric shade was printed using a delicate leaf motif – the same leaf stamp as used on the mirror surround (see page 76). For curved surfaces, you will need to roll the larger stamp around the profile of the shade to transfer the paint. Use acrylic colours for the shade and blend carefully to get just the right hue.*

On the stamped side table (see page 122), a fabric drawstring bag features the simple daisy stamp as used for the dressing table, although here it is seen without the interlocking border. Make your own bag up from a combination of fabric scraps or decorate a purchased one.

A rectangular piece of fabric decorated with a scalloped edge was sewn onto a circular base for this pretty bag. Two rows of stitches provide a channel for an organza drawstring ribbon, as well as holding the lining fabric in place.

BELOW. *A shaped plant pot holder and tissue box are decorated with a stamp that has featured elsewhere in the room (see page 123). Here you can see how a single stamp can be just as effective and decorative as a surface heavily patterned with stamps, as this planter clearly shows. A simple, lined edge (see page 31) provides a neat, crisp finish. The surface of both pieces is further enhanced by the* application of a delicate crackle varnish. Two-part varnish creates a fine network of cracks over the whole of the painted and stamped surface.

The cracks are clearly defined when a little burnt umber artist's oil colour is wiped over the surface with a soft cloth. And the oil colour will also subtly change the overall colour, giving it a rather faintly antiqued finish.

Both of these smaller accessories can be purchased as plain, undecorated 'blanks' made specifically for decorating purposes. You will find a number of companies that supply this type of furniture at the back of many home interest magazines and their prices are often very good as they offer a mail order service with no overheads. The tray was also a 'blank', but it was simply treated with a colour wash effect and small decoupage border.

RIGHT. *The wardrobe doors are patterned with a fleur de lys stamp (see page 122). First, the cupboard was painted with a creamy off-white base. The stamp was then printed, using acrylic colours, in a cool grey shade. Once the colours were dry, the whole wardrobe was rubbed (fairly vigorously) with a pad of steel wool and coloured antiquing wax* (see page 27). The wax deepens the base colour and enriches the matt paint surface, giving a soft, silky-smooth finish to the surface. This rubbing action also starts to remove some of the underlying paint and gives the surface an antique quality.

Fabric cushions are stamped with simple shapes. The spiral leaf stamp was the same as the one used for the picture frame (see page 81), and the larger base cushion features the delicate leaf stamp also used on the lampshade and the mirror surround (see pages 79 and 87). There are lots of stamps used here, even in this small corner of the bedroom, but at no time does the effect become too contrived or over-the-top.

The
BATHROOM

*G*enerously *proportioned bathrooms are something of a luxury item these days, but this is not a reason for compromise. This room combines natural fabrics with painted tongue-and-groove wall cladding, colour washed walls and mosaic tiles. Even in a small bathroom there are plenty of surfaces available for decorating – a tiled splashback or a small mirror frame, as well as larger items like cupboards, drapes and laundry bins. Wherever there's a plain surface, there's a place for a stamp.*

Window coverings can be a problem for hot, steamy rooms, but these shutters are combined with strong fabric panels rather than fussy curtains to give an effective solution. The fabric panels are tied onto a pole and decorated with a spiralling stamp – the same stamp as used for the cupboard doors. Stripes on the fabric are used to determine the width of the stamp. Make sure the drapes fall short of the floor as bathroom floors are inevitably wet, soggy affairs – at least in my household – and the fabric wouldn't look as good with a dark watermark at the hem!

Don't overcrowd your bathroom with too many different stamped designs. The patterns used here all link together, usually with a spiral or circle motif and this keeps the room from becoming too contrived or overbearing.

TILED SPLASHBACK

MATERIALS: *Steel tape measure, MDF or marine ply, marker pen, small saw, tile adhesive, tile spreader (if necessary), mosaic or regular tiles, tile spacers, sponge, powdered tile grout, filler knife, squeegee, cloth, stamps (see pages 120 and 124–125), black ceramic paint, saucer, methylated spirits or ceramic paint solvent, electric power drill fitted with a masonry bit, bradawl, Rawlplugs, four strong screws, a screwdriver and sealant.*

It's not difficult to make a tiled splashback for a small sink unit but you will need to use MDF (medium-density fibreboard) or marine ply as both of these surfaces will not warp or twist if wet.

Use a retractable steel tape measure to measure first the width of the area you are covering, then the height of the required splashback. Plot these measurements on your board and cut the board to size using a jigsaw or a hand-held saw, making sure your cutting lines are completely straight and the angles are perfect right angles. Mark the board with a strong marker pen before you start cutting, if necessary, and stick to this line. Once

the board is cut, you will need to fix on the tiles. You may use any kind of wall tiles for your splashback, but here I have chosen to use small mosaic tiles for a more interesting look. These are available from good tile suppliers but it is worth checking the phone directory to see what companies are in your area as swimming pool suppliers will usually have the best selection.

The tiles are fixed onto the board with a layer of thinly spread tiling adhesive. This should be applied with a knotched spreader, which will ensure that the adhesive is evenly dispersed. The tiles can then be fixed into place. If you are using mosaic tiles, these are pre-laid onto a paper-backed surface, which means that the grout spaces between each tile are exactly spaced. However, for regular tiles, you will need to use tile spacers between each tile to allow for the grout. These can be purchased easily and cheaply from your tile supplier.

When the adhesive is dry, the backing paper is soaked off (if mosaic tiles are used), and the whole surface is then grouted between the gaps. Once dry and wiped clean, the stamping can be done. Because of the nature of a splashback, the more durable the paint that is used for the stamp, the more hard-wearing the surface will be. Ceramic paints are ideal – emulsions or water-based paints will not stand up to any rough treatment.

Drill a hole through the splashback corners and position this on the wall. Mark four holes onto the wall by pushing a bradawl through the tile holes. Remove the splashback and drill holes using an electric power drill fitted with a masonry bit. Fill these holes with Rawlplugs, then replace the splashback, lining up the holes, and screw it back into position onto the wall. Finally, an individual tile is neatly positioned over each of the screw heads for perfect concealment.

1 Cut your splashback base board to size, (measure the width of the area you are covering) ensuring that the sides and angles are neatly cut. Then, to make a good fixing for the tiles, first scrape the base board all over with the edge of a small handsaw to scratch the smooth surface.

2 Next, using a knotched spreader, apply the tile adhesive all over the prepared board so that the whole area is covered. Spread the adhesive out evenly over the surface using the notched tool provided with the pack of adhesive, or you could use a 3 mm (⅛ in) notched spreader.

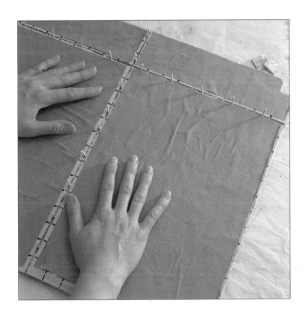

3 Press the tiles firmly to bed them onto the wet adhesive surface. Mosaic tiles can be laid directly over the grout, but if you are using regular tiles, then you will need to use tile spacers. Remember to leave a gap of one tile space in each corner of the board to allow for the screw fixings.

4 When the tile adhesive has dried out completely (refer to the manufacturer's instructions), you will need to remove the backing paper from the mosaic tiles. Wipe a damp sponge over the backing to soak it first, then wait a few minutes and peel the backing carefully away.

5 Mix up about four cupfuls of powdered grout (more if you need it) with enough water to make a soft consistency that looks rather like a raw cake mixture and spread this evenly over the whole of the tiled surface using an old filler knife. Roughly cover the whole surface of the board.

6 Use a rubber-bladed squeegee to press the grout deeply between the tile spaces and to remove any excess grout as you go along. Wipe the surface of the tiles with a damp cloth. As the grout begins to dry, wipe the tiles again until the whole surface of the board is completely clear.

RIGHT. *The finished tiled splashback needs to be sealed for watertightness with a line of transparent or white plastic sealant positioned between the bottom edge of the board and the back of the ceramic sink. This sealant is available in tubes from any decorating store or supplier. Occasionally, it is sold in a hard plastic tube and requires a metal trigger system. However, both types are easy to use and the seal will prevent water from seeping between the sink and the tiled splashback.*

When cleaning, wipe the surface with a damp cloth, rather than scrubbing it. The ceramic colour will be durable once it is dry, but it will deteriorate much more quickly if strong detergents are used.

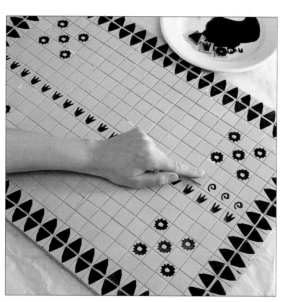

7 Make up the tiny stamps (as described on pages 32–33), but use a single mosaic tile as the backing. (A piece of wood this size would be much too tricky to cut as the stamp is so small.) Put some ceramic paint onto a saucer and apply this evenly to coat the stamp. Begin stamping the tiles.

8 Build up the pattern according to the design used here or create your own pattern with the stamps. Use ceramic colour (not the type that needs baking) to seal the colours (see page 19) and, when dry, fix the board firmly onto the wall with Rawlplugs, strong screws and a screwdriver.

BELOW. *The small mirror frame was first sanded down, then painted with two coats of an off-white emulsion colour. First of all, you will need to work out the number of stamps that will fit along each side of the mirror frame so that the stamps are printed evenly. Mark the positions of the stamps with a pencil. Print the stamps, then allow to dry (about 30 minutes). A black line was painted between each motif, using acrylic colour.*

When dry, the whole frame was rubbed with antiquing wax to deepen the colours and protect it. Any paint that is brushed onto the mirror can be scraped off with a Stanley knife blade. (For this motif, see page 120.)

RIGHT. *This large bathroom cupboard was originally a kitchen cupboard, but its Shaker look was perfectly suited to the style of this bathroom. Copious storage facilities meant that everything that was needed in the bathroom could be hidden away neatly, leaving only the most decorative bits and pieces on view. The stamp featured here is the same one as used on the curtain drapes (see page 90). Use emulsion paints and seal with at least two coats of acrylic varnish.*

The stamped design (see page 125) may also be repeated on the inside of the cupboard if you wish. You could even try switching the two colours around so that the inside becomes a creamy base colour with a blue stamped motif.

SHAKER LINEN BOX

I made this linen box using flexible plywood secured with metal rivets. The top and bottom were made from MDF (medium-density fibreboard) and then cut into a round shape using a jigsaw. To make the narrow band of ply around the top of the box lid, I used the same flexible ply as for the base and then stuck this around the MDF lid using strong wood adhesive. It was then panel-pinned for added security. A simple slot was cut into the centre of the lid, just wide enough to push a loop of hessian webbing through, to be used as the linen box handle.

Almost any size of container can be used following this procedure – tall and thin, or stumpy and shallow, according to your specific requirements. It may sound crazy but always make sure you'll be able to reach the bottom of the box when it's finished! This size of

MATERIALS: *Medium-grade abrasive paper, sanding block, box container of your choice, base coat colours (here I used a mid-tone blue, tinted with white for the top coat), 5 cm (2 in) paintbrush, wax candle, tailor's chalk, stamps (see pages 120 and 124), off-white stamp colour, cloth and clear acrylic varnish.*

container was about the right depth for me, but any deeper and there would have been a struggle to reach those linens right at the bottom.

The small stamps are evenly spaced around the outside of the box and some of the motifs that occur here are those used on the tiled splashback *(see pages 92–95)*. Scale the motifs up a little larger than those used before and secure the foam rubber as usual onto a timber block. I printed the motifs onto a colour-distressed background *(see page 25)* and used colours that were sympathetic to those seen in the bathroom; predominantly, the colours of the floor tiles. The off-white stamping colour was strong enough to register each small stamp, but not so powerful that the pattern became too important.

Other containers could be equally suitable for a linen box, provided the sides are smooth enough to stamp on. Wicker or Lloyd Loom types of box are not suitable for stamping as the open weave prevents the stamp from printing successfully.

The soft aqua blue shade, used to paint this linen box, complemented the other colours in the bathroom quite brilliantly. As only small amounts of paint are used, you will probably find that two tester pots of colour are sufficient for a linen box of this particular size.

It is always advisable to seal the paint effect prior to use, particularly in a bathroom as the damp conditions may spoil the finished container. Acrylic varnish is easy to use and the layers can be applied fairly quickly (within an hour at the most), making it easier to complete the whole project within a day.

An alternative to the webbing handle would be to fix a wooden drawer knob onto the top of the lid. This could then be painted and distressed in the same way as the rest of the container.

1 Prepare the container (if you are making it) or choose an undecorated linen box. Next, prime the base coat, lid and sides evenly and allow the paint to dry (about 30 minutes). Once the paint is thoroughly dry, rub over the whole of the painted surface with a wax candle.

2 Next, paint a second, much darker colour over the first shade of paint. You can afford to apply this layer in a rather uneven, patchy way as it will be distressed later on. Apply the second colour to both the sides and lid of the container in this way to cover the whole surface.

3 When the colours are fairly dry (about 30 minutes to an hour), you may find that some types of paint may still show signs of wetness over the heavily worked waxed areas and will not dry completely. Rub the surface of the box to distress it, using abrasive paper and a sanding block.

4 Stamp the motifs around the linen bin in the usual way. For even spacing and a regular pattern, you should first mark the positions of each stamp using white chalk. When dry (about 30 minutes), wipe away the chalk with a damp cloth and varnish to seal and protect the surface.

RIGHT. *The crown motif used on the Shaker linen bin also features along the edge of this hand towel. I cut a strip from a piece of checked fabric and stamped the motif inside the lighter-coloured squares to form an edging, which I then sewed onto a towel. Alternatively, a stamped edging strip could also be sewn along the hem of a bathrobe or around a flannel or bathmat to co-ordinate.*

The duckboard that you can see in both of the pictures opposite can be easily constructed using lengths of smoothly finished timber. These lengths are secured at the back with two battens that were cut from the same timber and sanded down thoroughly before decorating. I used duck egg blue for the base coat and cream emulsion for the spiral stamp (see page 125), then protected the surface with several coats of acrylic varnish, when dry (about 30 minutes), to make it water-resistant.

RIGHT. *The washbag and stool cover were made from practical cotton towelling, which can be purchased at good fabric outlets; alternatively, you could use a regular white towel. Lengths of stamped fabric edging (featuring the crown stamp once more) were used to decorate both the washbag and the cover (as for the hand towel). The washbag was made using two rectangles of fabric, sewn around three sides, catching a decorative trimming along the bottom. You could use tassels or fringing or sew fabric zigzags. A facing was sewn into the top of the bag and it was turned inside out. Parallel rows of stitches form a channel for the drawstring cord to pass through.*

Finally, a scalloped fabric edge was added to the sides of this stool cover before dropping it over the top of the stool for an instant transformation.

BELOW. *A junk find, such as this table, can make a useful surface for bathroom bits and pieces. This collection of pebbles with holes and dried seaweed creates an interesting still life, and the creamy ceramic fruit dish makes an interesting container for soaps and sponges. The table is simply prepared and painted white. I used white emulsion paint to cover the surface, and once dry (about 30 minutes to an hour), I printed a circular stamp (see page 120) around the edge of the table top to emphasize the pretty top, then sealed it with a coat of varnish.*

Plot the positions of the stamp before you start to avoid the last circle either being squashed up onto the first or a large gap appearing between the first and last stamp. Treat the top of the table as if it were a clock face: mark in the main positions, then fill in as many stamps between each quarter as will fit. Print the motif using a soft grey acrylic colour and emphasize the top further with fine lining to edge. Seal and protect the colours with varnish, when dry.

RIGHT. *These plain, undecorated containers are perfect surfaces for stamping. They can be used for almost any type of bathroom storage – cotton wool, make-up, toilet rolls or as planters for fresh flowers.*

I used a similar motif to the one used for both the curtain drapes and the wall cupboard (see page 125). However, the shape was made smaller and simplified a little. On a curved container, as in these three examples, you will need to roll the stamp over the surface to transfer the paint. Mark the positions of each motif prior to stamping. For a round container, you will find it easier to turn the pot upside down and to mark the positions of a clock face onto the base. Extend the markings around the sides of the container to give you the stamping guidelines.

Emulsion paint was used for the stamps and, once dry, I then sealed the inside of the planter pot using acrylic varnish to protect the absorbent wood from dampness.

The NURSERY

*H*and-painted cotton fabrics, stamped walls and furniture are all combined here in this really bright and cheerful room. Baby pinks or powder blues are strictly banished from this altogether far more exciting and stimulating nursery. Bed linen is just as important in this room as any piece of furniture or curtaining, and ordinary white cotton fabric is ideal for stamping. As well as saving yourself a fortune, hand-stamped fabric looks wonderful when made up into your own cot bumpers or used to trim the edge of a fitted chair cover. A simple heart stamp elevates a more humble fabric for these Roman blinds, and even a single heart-stamped panel, appliquéed onto cotton, lifts an otherwise dull cushion and chair cover.

The nursery walls were clad in a simple white-washed tongue-and-groove panelling and finished off with a practical peg rail. Above the wall cladding, wide magenta and white stripes were white washed and stamped with a floral motif to provide a calm background for the more decorative elements that accessorize the room.

Following on from this, the hearts and flowers theme is carried through and used on the storage unit. Stylized roses are stamped onto the drawer front and the back board of the unit. The shaped leaf is also featured around the flat sides of two storage trugs.

FOLK-ART COT BUMPER

Depending on the type of cot, it may be necessary to have pieces of foam cut for the sides, or it may be possible to cover a pre-fabricated cot bumper that has already been purchased. Either way, you must check very carefully that all the relevant safety tests have been carried out on any particular product. Foam mattresses and bedding have been linked with some research studies on infant cot deaths, so always purchase your materials from a reputable source and never buy anything without safety labels.

The foam sides are covered in a hand-painted and stamped fabric. Stripes are first drawn, then painted horizontally and vertically across the fabric to make a checked pattern. You will find it easier to paint if you tape the fabric over a flat surface first, placing absorbent paper between the fabric and the work surface. Use a ruler and a pencil first to measure and plot the positions of the stripes and join the lines together. Paint the stripes onto the fabric

MATERIALS: *Absorbent paper, masking tape, cotton fabric (enough to cover the bumper on both sides), long ruler, soft pencil, green fabric dye, fitch or wide stiff-bristled artist's brush, stamps (see pages 120 and 122), purchased foam bumper or foam pieces (cut according to your cot shape), green and red fabric paints, paper (for templates), tailor's chalk, dressmaker's pins, scissors, sewing needle, tacking thread, sewing thread, sewing machine, ironing board and iron.*

with powdered fabric dye that has been diluted in hot salted water. (Follow the manufacturer's recommendations for hand dying.) The colour may bleed a little at the edges of each stripe, but control this as much as possible by painting along the edge with light movements and work quickly. Once the edges of each stripe are painted in, the inside area can be filled in.

When the stripes are dry, the two stamps can be printed onto the fabric. Once the motifs are dry, the fabric is then ironed to seal in the colours and cut to size. Cut the stamps from foam *(see pages 32–33)*. The heart stamp is printed onto white squares positioned between the colour bands. Then, to create a gingham effect, the green stamp is printed over the intersection at each band.

Each piece is cut 2.5 cm (1 in) wider all round than the foam pieces for a seam allowance and to allow for fitting. A contrasting piping line is then inset between the fabric and foam for a tailored finish. The fabric is also sewn into a tie for each corner of the bumper and inserted between the two fabric pieces. When sewing the pieces together, leave a gap for turning through and filling, then hand sew to close the gap. Repeat the same procedure for all sides of the bumper. The pieces are then tied onto the sides of the cot and the mattress is replaced.

To add another pattern and colour, a contrasting cover has been made for the cot. Make the fabric ties from the same material. For each tie, cut two pieces of fabric with tapering ends. With right sides together, sew around the sides leaving a small gap for turning. Press, then sew the gap to close. Each tie is folded in half across the centre, then sewn into the sides of the bumper cover and tied around the sides of the cot. Each tie should measure approximately 30 cm (12 in).

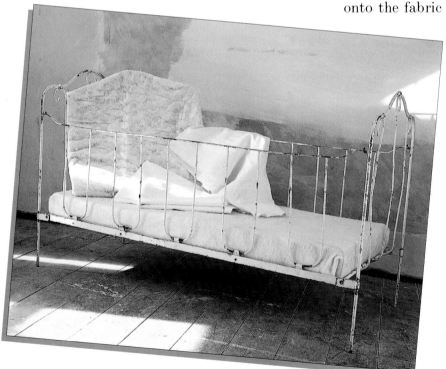

1 Place a layer of absorbent paper over a large work surface and then smooth and tape the cotton fabric over the top. (This protective paper layer will blot up any surplus fabric dye, once it has been applied.) When using large fabric pieces, it is easier to print one section at a time.

2 Use a long straight-edged ruler to mark out exactly the vertical positions of the stripes over the whole of the fabric section and then draw them in with a soft pencil mark. Once the verticals are plotted, then mark in the horizontals in the same way until the whole area is gridded up for painting.

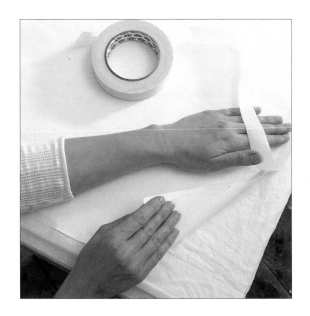

3 Next, mix up the fabric dye according to the manufacturer's instructions on the package. If the dye is warm, allow this to cool completely before using on the fabric. Use a fitch or wide, stiff-bristled artist's brush to brush on the dye, taking care not to let any of the outer edges 'bleed'.

4 When the dye has dried completely (refer to manufacturer's instructions), print the two different motifs over the whole of the fabric using the prepared blocks and following the pattern in the photograph. Use fabric paints for the printing, blending the colours together if necessary.

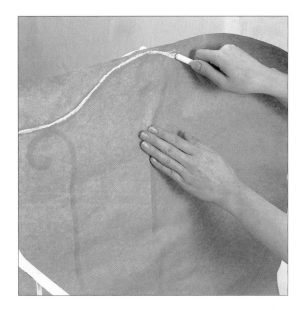

5 Make up the templates for each cot bumper section, using either pattern paper, brown paper or newspaper and following the shape of your foam pieces to mark out with tailor's chalk. If your cot pieces are more regular shapes, you may not need templates – just accurate measurements for each piece.

6 Lay each of the paper templates over the fabric, pin these together and then cut out the pieces for the sides of the cot. Make sure you add an extra 2.5 cm (1 in) all around to give a seam and turning allowance, and you will need to allow two pieces for each side of the cot bumper.

RIGHT. *Cot bumpers are not only decorative in a nursery, they can also help to keep your baby snug and safe. Always check with your hospital or midwife first to see whether cot bumpers are suitable for very young babies and children, as health studies relating to materials and fabrics in the nursery are being continually researched and the information is constantly being updated.*

The plain white, inexpensive fabric used here is hand painted and stamped to create a bold and cheerful pattern, which is then cut to shape according to the shape and size of your own cot.

Always purchase foam that is specifically designed for nursery use when making your own cot bumper. Bumpers that are purchased ready-made and only require covering with fabric should have been tested to the highest safety standards before being made available to the public. If in doubt, make sure you check the safety labels first before buying a bumper.

7 Turn the fabric pieces together so the right sides are facing one another. Pin the covered piping between these layers, keeping the raw edges together, and fit in a finished fabric tie at each corner. Tack and then machine sew the pieces together. (Remember to leave a gap for turning.)

8 Turn each of the bumper pieces to the right side through the turning gap. Press, then push the corners through and fill with the pieces of foam. Add the ties and then sew each of the gaps to close and secure the bumper onto the cot. Replace the mattress and cot cover.

RIGHT. *This blind was made up as described in the Bedroom chapter* (see pages 82–86). *It is a Roman blind and is raised and lowered using cords that are gathered at the side. Here the cord is hidden behind the curtain drape. The checked fabric for the blind was stamped with the same simple heart motif that was used on the cot bumper. It is easier to stamp the motif more accurately if it is cut to the same size as the white square in which it is then positioned. As the sides of the block register with the sides of the checked square, the heart motif is centred perfectly every time. Choose a thick cotton lining for this blind, as blocking out the light can often be an important consideration when you are planning out a nursery.*

RIGHT. *The single heart motif was printed onto a scrap of fabric. Once the edges were neatly turned under to make a square, the fabric was sewn onto a square of textured cotton fabric. This made up the front of a cushion cover* (for instructions for cushions, see page 72).

To make the chair cover, I laid a square of cotton over the chair, so that the fabric sides overlapped by about 7.5 cm (3 in). Tuck under the front corners and pin. The back was cut around the backrest and any raw edges were turned under and hand sewn, followed by the front corners. Four long strips of fabric made the ties. Pin each tie onto the cover. Hand sew together.

Cut a long frill from a piece of checked fabric 7.5 cm (3 in) wide and twice as long as three sides of the chair seat. Stamp the fabric and baste along the top edge. Hem the bottom, then pull the stitches to gather. Pin, then sew the frill onto the cover.

COUNTRY-STYLE WALL UNIT

MATERIALS: *Wall unit, two cloths, white acrylic primer, Household and 5 cm (2 in) paintbrushes, base and top coat emulsions (sage green and off-white), wax candle, medium-grade abrasive paper, grey acrylic colour, fine, long-haired artist's brush, stamps (see page 118), pink and green stamp paints, chalk and antiquing wax.*

This unit was purchased as a raw MDF (medium-density fibreboard) piece of furniture in an unfinished and unprimed condition (although there was one point that was definitely in my favour – it wasn't flat packed!) The first thing that needed to be done was to wipe the whole surface using a damp cloth to remove dust particles from the cut surface. This should be done outside if possible as the dust particles from MDF can be very dangerous if they are inhaled.

The unit was then prepared with a coat of white acrylic primer, which was applied to all the surfaces and inside

the drawer. Once this was dry (about 30 minutes), the paint finish is applied. A distressed colour effect was applied *(see page 25)* to give a softer 'country' finish, which would be more sympathetic to the stamped design. Apply the green base colour and, when this is dry (about 30 minutes), rub a candle over the surface in all directions. The flat sides of the cupboard are perfect for this type of distressed effect. Once the wax has been applied, a second coat of off-white paint is painted onto the unit. When this coat is dry (about 30 minutes) or nearly dry, as some areas of paint may not dry out fully because of the underlying wax, the paint layers can be rubbed back with abrasive paper. Do this gently at first, increasing the pressure on the paper if more colour needs to be rubbed back. Rub those parts of the unit that you would normally expect to receive the most wear and tear, such as around the drawer knobs or on the corners.

The flower stamps are cut from the foam using the motifs at the back of this book *(see page 118)*. Cut a block for both the flower and the leaf as these can be used alone or in conjunction with one another to produce almost any arrangement that you choose to create. Fine lining details *(see page 31)* are painted around parts of the unit: for this, use a little acrylic colour, thinned with water in a saucer, and apply the paint with a long-haired artist's paintbrush. Leave the lines to dry and apply the flower and leaf stamps following the design featured here or your own pattern.

Once the stamps are printed onto the surface of the unit, its 'newness' is knocked back slightly using antiquing wax. The wax penetrates through the absorbent surface of the paint and dulls the colour slightly. Rub the wax evenly over the surface, then buff it up to a dull sheen with a clean cloth or duster.

1 Once the unit is wiped clean and is completely free from dust, the whole surface can then be primed with white acrylic primer using a household paintbrush. When this is dry (allow about 30 minutes), apply one layer of your chosen base colour paint. (I used an off-white shade.)

2 Next, rub an ordinary household wax candle over the entire painted surface. Move the candle outwards in all directions, paying particular attention to the corners and around the drawer knobs as these will normally receive the most wear and tear and this will help the 'ageing' process.

3 With a 5 cm (2 in) paintbrush, apply the second top coat of paint over the base to cover the waxed surface. Leave this to dry for about an hour when most of the paint should be dry, but some areas (such as the corners and around the drawer knobs) will inevitably stay wet where there is a build-up of wax.

4 Rub medium-grade abrasive paper over the whole unit to wear away the top colour and allow the base colour to show through. The wax coat enables you to remove the top layer of paint easily without too much pressure, so do this gradually, checking as you go along.

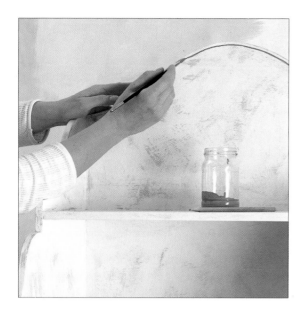

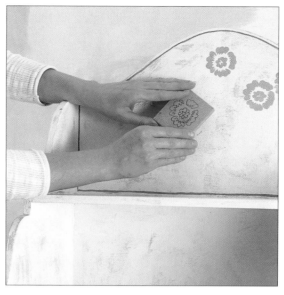

5 Use a little acrylic colour (here I used a shade of soft grey) to paint delicate lines around parts of the unit using a fine artist's paintbrush. The back board of this unit is a perfect place for the lining and I also added lining around the drawer front and sides for extra definition.

6 Load the flower motif stamp with pink paint first and print this over parts of the unit as required. Here the back board and the drawer front were stamped. You can assess the positions of each stamp by eye (if you feel confident to do so) alternatively mark them with tailor's chalk first.

RIGHT. *The finished cupboard is used to store all the cotton wool balls, creams, nappies and other paraphernalia that are required for a small baby. As a baby grows, the unit can be used for books and toy storage and if they throw it out when they become a teenager, well, reclaim it back into your own room!*

Children's rooms offer us a great opportunity to experiment with colour and patterns in a more liberating way perhaps than we would in our own rooms. Use these same flower stamps on a floor cloth, around a light fitting or a door frame. You could also stamp dull storage crates with bold colours and enjoy the effect of lots of differently patterned surfaces.

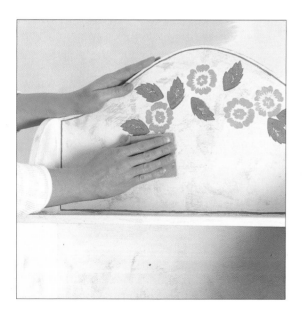

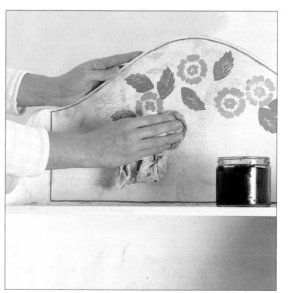

7 Load and stamp the leaf motif with green paint between the first flower stamps taking care not to overlap any parts of the design. Assess the overall effect by eye, adding another flower or leaf wherever appropriate. Again, mark out with tailor's chalk first, if you wish.

8 When all the colours are dry (allow about 30 minutes to an hour), rub a layer of antiquing wax over the surface of the cupboard. The brown tones of the wax deepen and enrich the emulsion paint and the wax buffs up to a silky smooth finish to complete the antiqued effect.

RIGHT. *Small trugs are invaluable for storing tissues, cotton wool and lotions – essentially all those small items that are used regularly in a nursery that otherwise seem to become misplaced or mislaid. The basic 'blank' was given a simple colour wash treatment (see page 22) using two similar emulsion colours. A single leaf stamp (see page 118), as featured on the larger trug, was used alone here, and the whole surface waxed with a coloured furniture wax (see page 25). This was applied with medium-grade wire wool, which not only adds body to the colours, but also distresses the paint surface so enhancing the country-style charm of this delightful nursery.*

The larger trug was given the same basic treatment, but the larger surface area benefits from using both stamps (see page 118).

RIGHT. *The nursery walls are painted in broad pink and white stripes, allowing the plaster shades of the wall beneath to 'ghost' through slightly. A stamp was applied (see page 122) following a regular pattern to achieve the hand-blocked effect.*

Padded hangers were made by wrapping a strip of wadding around a wooden hanger, tucking the ends in securely. A wide strip of stamped fabric was then sewn over, tucking the raw edges in and making small tucks to ease the fabric around the curve.

For the heart-shaped pouch, a stamped fabric heart was stitched onto a co-ordinating fabric and a heart shape was cut from this. A second heart was cut and the two pieces were then sewn together. The pouch was filled with wadding and lavender heads, then finished off with a button and raffia.

STAMP DESIGNS

SUPPLIERS

* Mail order available

UNITED KINGDOM

J.W. Bollom & Co. Ltd., 121 South Liberty Lane, Ashton Vale, Bristol BS3 2SZ.
Tel. (01179) 665151 Fax (01179) 667180
For paints.

*Brodie & Middleton, 68 Drury Lane, London WC2B 5SP.
Tel. (0171) 836 3289 Fax (0171) 497 8425
For supplies of theatrical materials.

*L. Cornelissen & Son Ltd., 105 Great Russell Street, London WC1B 3RY.
Tel. (0171) 636 1045 Fax (0171) 636 3655
For all gilding and artist's materials.

*Foxell & James, 57 Farringdon Road, London EC1M 3JB.
Tel. (0171) 405 0152 Fax (0171) 405 3631
For varnishes, stains and paints.

*Green & Stone of Chelsea, 259 Kings Road, London SW3 5EL.
Tel. (0171) 352 0837 Fax (0171) 351 1098
For paints, paint finishes, specialist brushes, fine art materials, cut-outs, water-based scumble and varnishes.

J.D. McDougall Ltd., 4 McGrath Road, London E15 4JP.
Tel. (0181) 534 2921 Fax (0181) 519 8423
For canvas, textile fabrics and hessian. Ring first for an appointment.

*John Mylands Ltd., 80 Norwood High Street, London SE27 9NW.
Tel. (0181) 670 9161 Fax (0181) 761 5700
For paints, waxes, brushes and varnishes.

*John S. Oliver Ltd., 33 Pembridge Road, London W11 3HG.
Tel. (0171) 221 6466 Fax (0171) 727 5555
For their own range of paint colours, fabrics and papers.

*London Graphic Centre, 16 Shelton Street, London WC2H 9JG.
Tel. (0171) 240 0095 Fax (0171) 831 1544
For fabric paints, graphics and artist's and architectural materials.

*Nutshell Natural Paints, Hamlyn House, Mardle Way, Buckfastleigh, Devon TQ11 0NR.
Tel. (013646) 42892 Fax (013646) 643888
For earth and mineral pigments, varnishes, natural paints and waxes.

*Papers & Paints Ltd., 4 Park Walk, London SW10 0AD.
Tel. (0171) 352 8626 Fax (0171) 352 1017
For specialist paints and glazes including historic and trade colours.

*Pentonville Rubber Products Ltd., 104/106 Pentonville Road, London N1 9JB.
Tel. (0171) 837 4582 Fax (0171) 278 7392
For 3 mm (⅛ in) thick foam rubber sheeting.

*E. Ploton (Sundries) Ltd., 273 Archway Road, London N6 5AA.
Tel. (0181) 348 0315 Fax (0181) 348 3414
For artist's and gilding materials and decorative effects.

*J.H. Ratcliffe & Co. (Paints) Ltd., 135a Linaker Street, Southport PR8 5DF.
Tel. (01704) 537999 Fax (01704) 544138
For scumble glazes, varnishes, tools and brushes, etc.

*Reed Harris, Riverside House, 27 Carnwath Road, London SW6 3HR.
Tel. (0171) 736 7511 Fax. (0171) 736 2988
For a range of wall and floor finishes, and unglazed mosaic tiles.

*Russell & Chapple Ltd., 23 Monmouth Street, Covent Garden, London WC2H 9DE.
Tel. (0171) 836 7521 Fax (0171) 497 0554
For canvas, hesssian and art materials.

*Scumble Goosie, Lewiston Mill, Brinscombe, Stroud, Gloucestershire GL5 2TB.
Tel. (01453) 731305 Fax (as phone)
For a range of MDF 'blanks', paints, plaster busts, etc.

UNITED STATES

*Pearl Art, Craft and Graphic Discount Centers; branches at all the following addresses:

308 Canal Street, NY, NY 10013
Tel. (212) 431 7932 and 1 800 221 6845 Fax (212) 274 8290. Orders: Pearl by Mail 1-800-451-Pearl (7327)

2411 Hempstead Tpke, East Meadow, NY 11544. Tel. (516) 731 3700 Fax (516) 731 3721. Orders: 516 579 6450

776 Route 17N, Paramus, NJ 07652
Tel. (201) 447 0300 Fax (201) 447 4102

6000 Route 1, Woodbridge, NJ 07095.
Tel. (908) 634 9400 Fax (908) 634 6851

2100 Route 38, Cherry Hill, NJ 08002.
Tel. (609) 667 6500 Fax (609) 667 6249

579 Massachusetts Avenue, Cambridge, Massachusetts 02139.
Tel. (617) 547 6600 Fax (617) 547 1906

12266 Rockville Pike, Suite P, Rockville, Maryland 20852.
Tel. (301) 816 2900 Fax (301) 816 4955

5695 Telegraph Road, Alexandria, Virginia 22303.
Tel. (703) 960 3900 Fax (703) 960 9130

3756 Roswell Road, Atlanta, Georgia 30342.
Tel. (404) 233 9400 Fax (404) 841 0382

1033 East Oakland Park Boulevard, Ft. Lauderdale, Florida 33334.
Tel. (305) 564 5700 Fax (305) 564 5715

4539 West Kennedy Boulevard, Tampa, Florida 33609.
Tel. (813) 286 8000 Fax (813) 286 0621

1140 East Altamonte Drive, Altamonte Springs, Florida 32701.
Tel. (407) 831 3000 Fax (407) 831 1042

6448 South Dixie Highway, South Miami, Florida 33143.
Tel. (305) 663 8899 Fax (305) 663 8382

6100 Westheimer Road, Suite 142A, Houston, Texas 77057.
Tel. (713) 977 5600 Fax (713) 977 4968
For a wide range of art supplies.

AUSTRALIA

The Folk Art Studio, 200 Pittwater Road, Manly, NSW 2095.
Tel. (02) 977 7091
For a wide range of craft materials including wooden items.

*Janet's Art Supplies, 145 Victoria Avenue, Chatswood 2067, Sydney.
Tel. (02) 417 8572 Fax (02) 417 7617
For a wide range of general art supplies.

*Oxford Art Supplies Pty Ltd, 221–223 Oxford Street, Darlinghurst 2010, Sydney.
Tel. (02) 360 4066 Fax (02) 360 3461
For general art supplies.

BIBLIOGRAPHY AND FURTHER READING

Ballantine, Belinda. *The Decoupage Kit*, London, Little, Brown & Company, 1993

Ballantine, Belinda. *The Furniture Painting Kit*, London, Little, Brown & Company, 1995

Barker, Linda. *Simply Paint*, London, Collins & Brown Publishers, 1993

Barker, Linda. *Simply Fabric*, London, Collins & Brown Publishers, 1993

Barker, Linda. *Simply Paper*, London, Collins & Brown Publishers, 1994

Barker, Linda. *Simply Stencilling*, London,

Collins & Brown Publishers, 1994

Barker, Linda. *Simply Colour*, London, Collins & Brown Publishers, 1994

Barker, Linda. *Simply Curtains*, London, Collins & Brown Publishers, 1995

Barker, Linda. *Making Cushions*, London, Salamander Books, 1995

Barker, Linda. *Just Junk*, Newton Abbot, David & Charles Publishers, 1997

Cavelle, Simon. *The Encyclopedia of Decorative Paint Effects*, London, Headline, 1994

Drucker, Mindy & Finkelstein, Pierre. *Recipes for Surfaces*, London, Cassell, 1992. Also pub. in USA, Running Heads Inc. , 1990

Innes, Jocasta. *Paintwise*, London, Pyramid, 1991

McCloud, Kevin. *Kevin McCloud's Decorating Book*, London, Dorling Kindersley, 1990

Sloan, Annie & Gwynn, Kate. *The Complete Book of Decorative Paint Techniques*, London, Century Hutchinson, 1988

INDEX

Page numbers in *italics* refer to illustrations

Acknowledgements

AUTHOR'S ACKNOWLEDGEMENTS

With many thanks to all those at Eddison Sadd who have helped to get this book to press, and to Lizzie Orme whose photography is truly inspirational.

EDDISON·SADD EDITIONS

Commissioning Editor	Zoë Hughes
Project Editor	Jane Donovan
Proofreader	Nikky Twyman
Indexer	Dorothy Frame
Art Director	Elaine Partington
Senior Art Editor	Sarah Howerd
Designers	Lynne Ross and Shefton Somersall-Weekes
Photographer	Lizzie Orme
Line Illustrations	Anthony Duke
Production	Hazel Kirkman and Charles James

PICTURE CREDITS

The photographs on page 7 are reproduced by kind permission of Arthur Sanderson and Sons Ltd.